LOST
GOLD RUSH TOWNS
—— OF ——
SACRAMENTO

T0384287

LOST
GOLD RUSH TOWNS
— OF —
SACRAMENTO

SPECIAL COLLECTIONS OF THE
SACRAMENTO PUBLIC LIBRARY

THE
History
PRESS

Published by The History Press
Charleston, SC
www.historypress.com

Manufactured in the United States

ISBN 9781467151139

Library of Congress Control Number: 2024949771

In loving memory of Clare Ellis (1949–2024), the founding manager and forever heart and soul of the Sacramento Room.

For Andrew's parents, Don and Susan; wife, Miriam; and kids, Devorah and Gabriel.

For Eric's wife, Colette; and father, Donald Webb.

For James's wife, Lori.

CONTENTS

ACKNOWLEDGEMENTS

We are grateful for the meaningful contributions made by several colleagues, organizations and community members in the creation of this book.

First, a massive thanks to the Sacramento Region Community Foundation. Without its kind financial assistance, this project could not have taken place.

Our acquisitions editor Laurie Krill from The History Press was such a pro—patient, instructive and ever so supportive.

Our Sacramento Public Library (SPL) colleagues, branch supervisors Jason Weekley and Christopher Curran, contributed significant amounts of research to make this book a reality.

Doing amazing things within a world-class network of Capital Area cultural heritage institutions, we thank Senior Archivist Kim Hayden and Archivist Nicholas Piontek of the Center for Sacramento History (CSH); Archives and Records Center Coordinator Heather Lanctot of the Yolo County Library (YCL); Folsom History Museum (FHM) Manager Shelby Sorensen and historian Rodi Lee; Photo Archivist Rebecca Crowther, Cultural Resources Program Manager and Museum Curator Dr. Emma Silverman and Museum Technician Judy Russo of California State Parks (CSP); and Librarian Melissa Foote of the California State Library's California History Section (CSL).

We also thank the reproduction staff at the University of California–Berkeley's Bancroft Library (UCB) and the University of California–Santa Barbara's Library and Geospatial Collection (UCSB). We are grateful to the

U.S. Geological Survey (USGS), California State Archives (CSA), Library of Congress (LOC), California Department of Transportation (CalTrans) and the Society of California Pioneers (SCP) for their assistance. Please note that institutional abbreviations will be used for photograph and map attribution throughout the book.

Lastly, we are grateful for our patrons, who drive us to get better every day. Together, we are an irrepressible force for illumination.

INTRODUCTION

Sacramento is haunted by missing cities. Ghost towns litter the Old West, but something spookier happened here: Entire towns were wiped off the map along a broad swath of land flanking the American River. "Lost Sacramentos" are different than the veins of older buildings often found embedded in a growing metropolis and distinct from the rustic mining towns where boom and bust left iconic remnants standing like tombstones. Lost Sacramentos vanished, almost completely, under suspicious circumstances.

Each disappearance was different. We still know the names of Sutterville, Brighton and Prairie City, whose names drift vaguely around Sacramento's edges. But Norristown and Hoboken have entirely faded from memory, leaving only blocked roadways and kinked property lines. Mormon Island and Negro Hill suffered more ordinary declines before they were drowned in Folsom Lake, their marginalized founders erased from history.

Lost Sacramentos died in various ways, but the frequency and consistency with which they vanished raises questions. This book seeks answers.

The region's pattern of losses suggests an unusual process of arrested development, which historians have so far failed to adequately explain. Many miles of choice riverfront were left uninhabited, along with the land corridor between Sacramento City and the first gold strike in Coloma. The channels through which one of history's greatest flows of humanity once coursed went mysteriously dry. Where we might ordinarily expect strings of historic settlements, there are instead only sparse remnants of Sacramento's first century as an artery of American resource extraction.

Details of these disappearances remain elusive, but clearly something significant is missing. And the following survey of Lost Sacramentos will unearth a disturbing string of clues pointing toward Sacramento City, the survivor that formed the core of the modern city called Sacramento. This solitary land scheme apparently stands alone as a result of actions that actively removed its competitors from the field, over time frames ranging from days to decades. These hypothetical removals are still mostly unknown but presumably intentional, and most likely they are connected to the region's intense and briefly bloody struggle for land and riches.

Typical gold rush landownership conflicts surely account for some properties being seized and repurposed, but missing documents impede proper understanding of this tumultuous time. While these gaps in the historic record have likewise escaped proper scrutiny, details around their edges provide tantalizing hints of a disturbing scenario in which records were intentionally removed—along with the communities they recorded. Not every disappearance fits a single explanation, and conditions vary significantly across the transition from the Sacramento River to the foothills. Some towns were gone even before the gold rush ended. Others had more typical declines before their memory was sanitized in the service of a white Protestant settler mythology, their remnant infrastructure submerged by the ongoing project of protecting Sacramento City from almost inevitable flooding.

In any case, half a dozen gold rush towns are gone, and their disappearance calls for investigation. This book's authors are just beginning to understand who removed these towns and how they did it. However, the answer seems rooted in Sacramento City's origins as a controversial, turbulent real estate scheme in which speculators sought any opportunity to "mine the miners." Another element is the racist and religiously exclusive narrative that has dominated Sacramento storytelling through most of the historic period. Yet another is the profit motive that drove company towns to grow only until they ceased to support the right bottom line. And a central thread appears to be Sacramento City's need to manage its fatal flaw, protecting land investments by stopping floods at all costs. We hope to encourage further critical inquiry into an emerging historic mystery.

While this book primarily recalls struggle that took place among white settlers, it also raises the essential question of what happened to people on the other side of California's brutal racial divide. The promise of Anglo settler "civilization" was rooted in orderly systems of private landownership, but the failure to develop a durable community in some of this region's best locations punctures that romantic notion: The American intruders took some of the Indigenous Nisenan people's most precious land and then couldn't even figure out who owned it. So they cleared it out, with a second dispossession leaving the place empty and forgotten. Any surviving Nisenan must have been baffled and heartbroken.

And if entire towns full of mostly white folks might vanish, how could settlers of color possibly hold their ground? The intra-community racial dynamics of Lost Sacramentos are only briefly discussed in the following pages. The present work also stops short of a necessary study of smaller communities of color that were cleared away—whether known or unknown to history. Points of entry for such inquiry hide in plain sight: Negro Bar appears clearly on the plat of Folsom, the railroad town that obliterated it.[1] And there must be a good reason why a 1911 topographic map identifies "N****r Slough" alongside the route of a missing major road north from Sacramento, at a spot where marginalized settlers might have once hoped to avoid the worst of the largely white-on-white land drama south of the river.[2] These stories must be told as part of California's commendable but long-overdue reckoning with race and reparations. And we hope that this book provides a foundation for that essential research by showing the scale of loss that even white settlers suffered here.

The Lay of the Land

Sacramento sprang forth at a geographic chokepoint of one of history's greatest migration events, with great crowds chasing the planet's richest gold strike to date. This was approximately the center of a broad stretch of valley whose rivers drained fantastically rich mineral deposits, and Sacramento City was carved out of swamplands supposedly granted to Johann Augustus Sutter—against his will, ironically enough. The scheme's promoters exploited fresh-off-the-boat Johann Sutter Jr., whose best efforts to help manage his old man's torturous portfolio did more harm than good. Nevertheless, speculators led by Samuel Brannan sought and ultimately attained hegemony over a key crossroads connecting the port and financial center at San Francisco, the overland trails from the east and global dreams of sudden and fabulous wealth.

Sacramento City's solitary waterfront was about as far as a cargo-laden ship could consistently sail up the Sacramento River. Here, "Sutter's Embarcadero" hunkered on a glorified sandbar between the river and a flood basin just below the confluence with the American River, whose banks offered reasonably good land routes into the hills. This was an excellent place for a resource extraction hub. It was also an awful place to live, but people sure gave it a good try.

Sacramento City was only one of a cluster of settlements on the land that became Sacramento—the two place names must not be confused. The modern city sprang from a decentralized web of increasingly American settlement, a cluster of competing schemes to cash in on the land corridor broadly known as the Coloma Road, which roughly followed the south bank of the American River. People flooded in from everywhere, and they all had to live and work somewhere. Sacramento was an ideal location in which to set up shop and wait for whatever gold others scratched out of the Mother Lode. This was a lucrative location for anyone with food, tools, booze or sex to sell, especially if they had some real estate on which to hang their shingle. Intense competition and political turmoil added to the challenges of establishing who owned what. Land values skyrocketed as surging crowds of miners and settlers fueled the rapid growth of numerous towns.

This unruly immigrant horde settled anywhere and everywhere, but only one town survived to become the core of California's lopsided capital. Here, many thousands of lots lured hapless investors into some of the most hazardous terrain of a generally hazardous landscape. Sacramento City was plagued by repeated flooding as well as land conflicts that exploded into violence in August 1850, when the "Squatters' Riot" caused the deaths of eight people, including the sheriff and assessor. The mayor was gravely wounded and fled town, never to return.[3] Sacramento City was a difficult and dangerous place, and yet in a land with two rivers and numerous potential waterfronts, this deeply flawed competitor is the sole survivor. Its erstwhile neighbors are gone and mostly forgotten.

Lost Gold Rush Towns of Sacramento will raise more questions than it answers. But we hope that our inquiry breaks a trail through thick historic undergrowth, to be followed by future researchers. As the United States wrestles with a boom of political disinformation, deepfakes and artificial intelligence, Americans must seriously consider how and whether unpleasant—or fictional—events are enshrined as history. Sacramento holds some hard lessons. The gold rush thus provides an urgent warning of the extent to which lies and amnesia can replace truth and memory. The forgetting of these lost towns shows that entire communities can be removed from history and memory.

The Disappeared City

Lost Sacramentos were not the typical suburban competitors absorbed by a stronger neighbor, reduced to a quaint streetscape or historic waterfront embedded in a larger metropolis. Nor were they the usual ephemeral mining camp. Around Sacramento, we find something different: Although the region was a relatively stable center of gold rush wealth generation, several entire city street grids disappeared—along with hundreds or even thousands of parcels. These vanished communities were home to numerous individuals who thought that they had acquired a secure toehold from which to do business and build a life. But their communities were somehow dismantled and forgotten.

The land of these dispossessed Sacramentans was already stolen, of course. Sacramento once belonged to the Nisenan, a people who were intimately familiar with the land and knew how to pick a settlement site. This culture's homeland stretched north and east into the foothills, varying significantly with elevation. In the lowlands, they were drawn to high riverbanks, where they sometimes built mounds to gain critical elevation above the flooding that made this valley both hazardous and sublimely abundant.

The Nisenan lived at ground zero of the gold rush, and they were hit hard and fast by the California genocide. Very little of their world and culture survives. Although mounds still mark old village sites in a few places, the Nisenan were all but obliterated. Lost Sacramentos compounded that tragedy, as our "civilized" society ironically failed to deliver on its promises of orderly landownership. The Nisenan at least knew which prime fishing spot belonged to whom.

The disappearance of Sacramento City's neighbors is often attributed to problems with the title chains that established legal landownership. But even in the "Wild West," dissolution of an entire established city should have left a massive paper trail and drawn much interest from journalists and historians. The process would have required either large-scale land condemnation or someone buying up every single parcel in town and then convincing the county to vacate any rights of way. Either scenario would have been loudly controversial, as land conflicts were usually a matter for passionate and detailed discussion in newspapers of the day. Alas, large swaths of newspapers are missing, along with the first twenty years of the county assessor's map books. These gaps are unfortunate and suspicious, and they have left a fundamentally flawed perception of the historic landscape.

Each of Sacramento City's rivals had its own shortcomings. They all faced varying challenges, including hazardous rivers and contested landownership. It is no surprise that some failed. But usually urban failures leave telltale remnants, like the Gold Country's charming and crumbling historic streetscapes. Where are such remnants in the lowlands? Under ordinary circumstances, old cores of towns would remain embedded in modern urban fabric. Instead, we usually see almost nothing. Boomtowns reverted to undivided farmland and then lay silent for decades. Some of the best places to live were emptied out and left nearly vacant. Lost Sacramentos could have contributed secondary urban centers, reducing the modern city's vulnerability to flooding. These communities would have helped build a more resilient modern city. Sacramento could have been less dependent on an urban center that grew in one of the worst possible locations.

These quiet disappearances would be strange enough if they had yielded a more robust pattern of settlement. However, the results of these changes were generally negative—both individually and in aggregate: Sites with the worst flooding and ownership controversies should have been abandoned. Instead, settlers were offered fewer and poorer choices as time went on.

These Lost Sacramentos will be considered sequentially in the following chapters, beginning on the valley floor and moving uphill toward the gold.

Sutterville was the oldest city in California's interior, predating Sacramento City by years and expanding significantly in 1850. Only a few fragments of its massive grid survived despite this being the preferred city site of the person whose title was supposedly the basis for all property claims in the area.

Brighton was located several miles up the American River from Sacramento City. This was government land just outside even the absurdly extended boundaries of Sutter's grant. The town's plat was one of the earliest maps recorded by Sacramento County. Sheriff McKinney was killed here on day two of the Squatters' Riot, and land conflict continued through most of a decade.

Norristown, and later Hoboken, stood just downstream of Brighton during the early 1850s, mostly on land that later became the Sacramento State University campus. Settlement attempts continued here for at least a decade. This prime location was a superb riverfront with high banks and slow, deep water. It went the way of Brighton despite a title chain clearly linking back to Sutter himself.

Meanwhile in the hills, Mormon Island and Negro Hill were cross-river neighbors at a lucrative gold strike on the El Dorado county line. Both were built by settler groups who were outsiders for religious or racial reasons. Despite their serious difference—especially Mormon slaveholding—each of these groups had strong traditions of mutual aid that hint at a range of ideas about communities and economics. Both faded from history long before they were flooded out by the creation of Folsom Lake.

Prairie City was a major settlement south of Folsom, just inside the eastern edge of Afro-Caribbean pioneer William Liedesdorff's Mexican grant. Although this town was home for hundreds of people through much of the 1850s, it too was wiped off the map and mostly forgotten until freeway construction disrupted its cemetery.

Lost Sacramentos each disappeared differently, suggesting a variety of removal processes. For example, no maps of Norristown survive, but traces survive to the present day in parcel boundaries that refer explicitly to the place. In contrast, a parcel map of Brighton can be easily viewed at the county assessor's public computer terminals—or even downloaded from the Internet—but the location it so precisely depicts is a matter of educated guesswork. Each of these settlements met its own peculiar demise, yet their shared disappearance connects them. And to understand this string of disappearances, we must first understand the large and ruthless neighbor that muscled them aside.

—ANDREW MCLEOD

CHAPTER 1

THE CANNIBAL CITY

By Andrew McLeod

It is a wonder that Sacramento City survived. Relentless waves of inundation marred its early years in a land of extraordinary flood hazard—a so-called inland sea. The modern city's arrangement is now taken for granted, but it was not a foregone conclusion. Although obscured by years of revisionist history as well as a dramatic physical transformation through flood control—a critical reading of Sacramento history reveals something seriously amiss in the early growth of the town that became California's capital: Rather than coexisting with its environment and its neighbors in less precarious locations, Sacramento City apparently cannibalized nearby waterfronts, throwing up levees and drawing much of the region's economic energy and human community into its own swampy grid. Notorious speculators like Samuel Brannan built a cutthroat culture of unscrupulous impunity here, and it seems that this notorious Wild West ethic operated at the intercity level too.

River cities typically feature multiple waterfronts. Consider Pittsburgh, Portland or Kansas City—dense development grows from multiple historic neighborhoods strung along the banks.[4] The same is true worldwide, from Baghdad to Bangkok. Even Bend, Oregon, boasts a longer and more complex waterfront than Sacramento, which hosted one of history's most dramatic explosions of river traffic. Here, navigable water from the Pacific ended at a river with nearly mythical golden allure. We should expect to find would-be settlers clinging to every root protruding from the city's many miles of riverbank. Obstacles like riparian marshes might have slowed development, but such problems rarely stopped the surge of settlers to any waterfront that erupted in the right place at the right time. Pioneers raised the oldest parts of Seattle's waterfront.[5] Sacramento City did the same, at least in some places. So why doesn't California's capital city simply bristle with riverfront neighborhoods?

Apparently Sacramento City ate the neighbors, starting with its birthplace at Sutter's Landing—a site now covered by an unremarkable city park, half a mile from the water. Although lacking the grisly horror of the Donner Party's literal cannibalism, the consumption of Lost Sacramentos was driven by the same calculus: In desperate straits, the strong may consume the weak in order to acquire energy from other bodies in order to survive until circumstances improve. Or perhaps a more apt analogy would be panicked shipwreck survivors clambering over one another's bodies to reach a lifeboat. Either way, it's a grim origin story.

But the unsettling fact remains: Only one old embarcadero can be found along nearly one hundred miles of the Sacramento River's eastern bank, which provided water access to some of the nineteenth century's most attractive land. The American River has no port facilities whatsoever.

Sacramento's retreat from its rivers is especially bizarre given the region's topography. The land is not as notoriously flat and featureless as generally thought. Valley floor riverbanks are built up on sediment deposits called levees.[6] These primordial banks still persist despite Sacramento's dramatically altered landscape and are ideal foundations for the artificial structures of the same name. Even today, the central city's highest lands hug the river north of downtown, with Old Sacramento perched on a much smaller levee. Incidentally, a similar landscape exists along the southernmost Mississippi River, where thin fingers of land sink slowly into the Gulf of Mexico. Those levees are visible even from space. New Orleans took root along this high ground, growing organically from a river bend much like the one hosting Sacramento's Front Street. But Sacramento City grew in a different direction, following a single grid blindly down into the swamps. There would be no Mexican Quarter.

And Sacramentans should have known better. The city's early history was punctuated by both routine and disastrous flooding, and reducing or escaping this threat was the top priority of development. Nevertheless, downtown now largely sits in a flood basin, while numerous alternatives—including those described in the pages to come—have been mostly obliterated despite commanding higher ground. The survival of Lost Sacramentos would have yielded a metropolis with reduced vulnerability

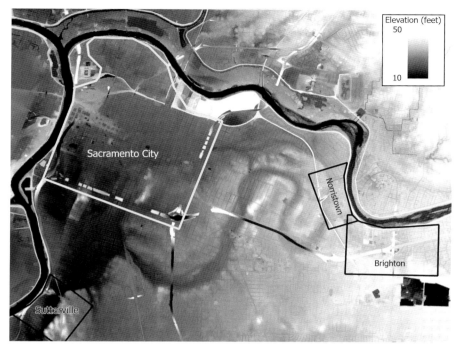

Sacramento's terrain is illuminated by this modern LiDAR image (*USGS*). Visible artificial structures include the rail levee that dramatically reshaped floodwater flow. *Andrew McLeod*.

to flooding, with more centers, improved density distribution and better transportation connectivity.

Sacramento supposedly began with "Sutter's Embarcadero," the famous tourist waterfront known as Old Sacramento State Historic Park. But in reality, settlement sprang from numerous locations connected to two great streams of water and humanity: The American River brought the gold, while the Sacramento River brought people, as well as the imports they needed to reach the gold. Newcomers arrived by distinct routes and tended to stop traveling at places that were attractive but not already taken. Many seekers came by ocean and river via San Francisco. Overlanders approached from the northeast, with their final obstacle the American River.

The region's earliest pathways and settlements were captured by General George Riley's 1849 map, *The Sacramento Valley from the American River to Butte Creek*. River roads are the dominant pathways. Except for the town of Sutter, settlement clusters along the American River. Riley exaggerated the hole in which this grid was located, which it shared with smaller subdivisions that

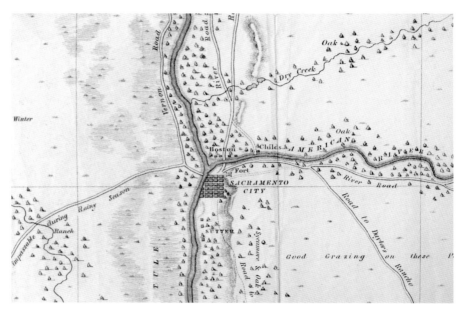

Part of General George Riley's map, *The Sacramento Valley from the American River to Butte Creek* (1849), depicting early land routes. *SPL.*

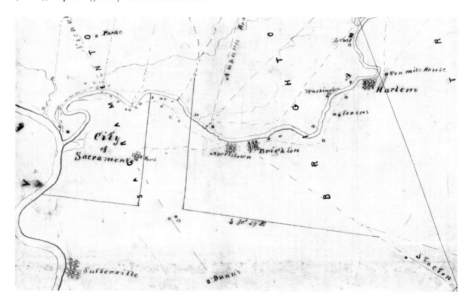

Deputy County Surveyor A.W. Thompson recorded the region's 1851 road network, showing how much travel followed the south bank of the American River. *CSL.*

apparently predated it. And Sacramento City's lowland terrain is not so flat as it appears to the casual observer—a few feet of elevation made a huge difference when the water came. Some parcels, especially along the rivers, were reasonably buildable, while others were often or always saturated.

The region's road network maintained roughly the same form until March 1851, when Sacramento County Deputy Surveyor A.W. Thompson apparently attached his name to a map depicting a different order—with Sutterville, Norristown and Brighton clearly shown. Different township boundaries created a buffer east of Sacramento City, while Brighton Township extended north to the county line. Despite these political surprises, growth evidently continued along a riverside axis, passing squarely through the Norristown and Brighton waterfronts. Roads to Sutterville were strangely absent, however, casting some doubt on overall accuracy; these must have existed. But overall, the Riley and Thompson maps depict a plausible progression of traffic patterns over two years of the gold rush.

The Grid's Rough Edges

Sacramento City was not just the tidy grid that first meets the eye. Nearly one thousand uniform blocks were surveyed around older communities at natural entryways. These predecessors appear plainly on the *Plan of Sacramento City*, which sprawls outward from two sets of irregular parcels located at exactly the best locations at which to greet (and fleece) newcomers. When this scheme was mapped out in 1848, its schemers most likely ate, slept, negotiated and caroused on this pair of northern waterfronts.

Despite the American River's central importance to Sacramento's founding, this second stream is strangely invisible in early images of Sacramento City. The first "bird's-eye" depictions offer roughly the same view of a nearly featureless riverbank. An 1857 map gives a much broader view of a growing city but is careful to crop out whatever was growing at the confluence.

It turns out there was a lot to see on the north side of town. The American River was rerouted during the 1860s, removing a pair of bends that were thought to increase the flood threat. This dramatic restructuring separated these two strategic waterfronts from their water. That same decade saw construction of a massive railroad levee well back from the banks on B Street; this blocked floodwaters from their ancient course down into the basin in which most of Sacramento City's real estate lay. Some of the area's

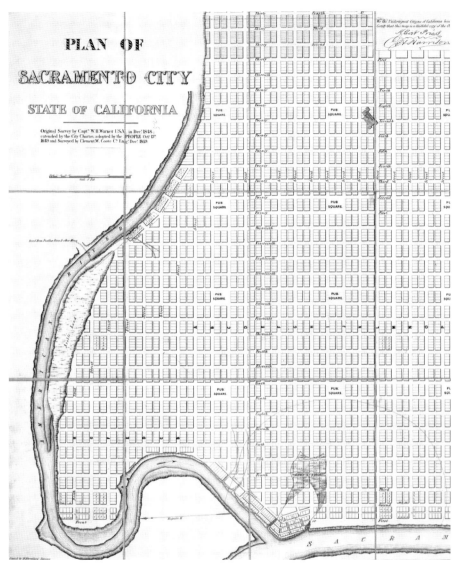

Above: Part of *Plan of Sacramento City* (1848), showing the city's northern half, including American River waterfront neighborhoods that probably predated the main grid. *LOC.*

Opposite, top: *Sacramento City, CA.* (1849) by G.V. Cooper provides a very constrained view of Sacramento's waterfronts, showing only a few blocks of "Old Sacramento." *LOC.*

Opposite, bottom: Part of *A Birds-Eye View of Sacramento* by George H. Baker (1857) offers a wider view but still excludes anything north of Sutter Lake. *CSH.*

oldest and best property thereby wound up both waterless and on the wrong side of the levee, cut off from the river's benefits but exposed to its hazards.

Meanwhile, Sacramento City literally looked the other way, turning its back on a pair of neighborhoods that most likely predated the larger city.

The first was El Calle de los Americanos, which stretched for five blocks just upstream of the main river crossing at 16th Street—the only point of entry labeled on the original city map. This waterfront's origins and people are unknown, but the name could not more strongly suggest a street

This 1880 depiction of Holland Farm in Thompson & West's *History of Sacramento County, California* provides an extraordinarily rare glimpse of the American River. *SPL.*

populated by Americans during California's pre-1848 Mexican period. This hottest of properties was the last stop on the long road to Sutter's Landing and, by 1851, the site of Lisle's Bridge. The 1854 city map showed that El Calle had expanded downstream to 10th Street. Today, a parallel road called Vine Street is the only trace of the settlement that first greeted overland arrivals en route to Sutter's Fort.

The Sacramento River was bridged years later, with a span that connected to the other disappeared settlement. While the Yolo side of the bridge connected near the center of Washington (now West Sacramento), the Sacramento side accessed the other side of the Sutter Lake outflow, near the confluence. This eastern approach was called Broad Street, an axis of a forgotten waterfront called Slater's Addition, just outside the frame of the 1857 depiction shown earlier. This angular neighborhood was probably named for an early city councilor who claimed to own its underlying land.[7] The eight-block strip consisted of three slightly different subdivisions, of varying depth and design. This diversity could indicate several owners making a loosely coordinated effort to cash in on the real estate boom exploding around them, or perhaps a preexisting settlement that had grown

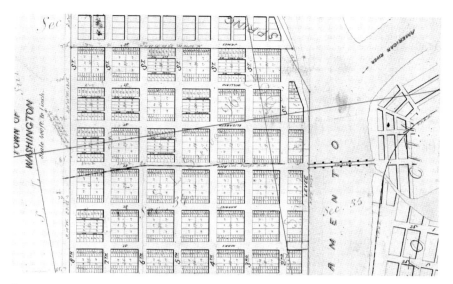

Part of *Town of Washington* (1869), which shows the 1857 Sacramento-Yolo Bridge connection to Slater's Addition. *Record of Maps Book A. Acc. #1989-012, YCL.*

Augustus Koch's 1870 bird's-eye includes Slater's Addition, showing the second bridge, an industrial waterfront and many houses along the former bank of the American River. *CSH.*

The Sacramento Gas Works was built on First Street in Slater's Addition, alongside structures possibly still buried in the levee (1854). *CSH.*

organically. It was also called the "American Fork Addition," but nobody knows the place's name before it was added to Sacramento City. Its remains are now buried in a levee just north of the I Street Bridge, and the most prominent surviving elements are ruins of the city's 1854 gas works, which appeared in an 1870 bird's-eye view along with the Pioneer Mill and a row of houses stretching along the American River's former mouth.

And then there was Boston, which shared the American Fork's northern riverbank with Pujune, where perhaps eight hundred Nisenan people once lived.[8] Despite this book's geographic focus south of the river, disappearances were not limited to its left bank. "Boston" is clearly marked on at least one version of the original Sacramento City map, on the peninsula just across the mouth of the American.[9] Boston was also located by Riley and mapped in detail on U.S. Navy Commander Cadwalader Ringgold's 1852 *Chart of the Sacramento River*. This navigational chart includes an inset labeled, "[P]art of the River Sacramento showing the location of the cities of Sacramento and Boston."[10] This map claims twin cities, which was a stretch. Although evidently flood-prone, Boston's eastern part also featured high land, just off the main overland route connecting Sacramento to the United States and the northern gold fields. It could certainly have been a paper town, yet Edmund Gould Buffum described blocks of 240 by 320 feet being at least partly occupied in 1850.[11] Boston was apparently well forgotten by 1886, when the baffled *Record Union* declared it to be "almost like a fiction" but still acknowledged the accounts of "pioneers, who remember the long rows of white tents."[12]

Title Troubles

Although its neighbors may have had title issues, Sacramento City's ownership controversies were severe. As Mark Eifler explains in *Gold Rush Capitalists: Greed and Growth in Sacramento*, doubts about Johann Augustus Sutter's Mexican grant were the root of serious and widespread conflict. Not only did this conflict spark a deadly armed uprising whose casualties included three public officials, it also helped precipitate a dramatic collapse in real estate values that was particularly troublesome due to a general practice of collateralizing inbound shipments with overvalued land.[13]

The Sutter dispute was entangled in a larger controversy over who owned what in California. The treaty ending the United States' war with Mexico established that valid grants would be respected, but Sutter's desperate financial straits and frequent inebriation led him into spectacularly unscrupulous and sloppy business affairs. He often sold land he did not own. To complicate matters, his twenty-three-year-old son arrived from Switzerland, and the two each made uncoordinated and sometimes duplicate sales. So did their various agents. So several claimants could each sincerely believe—with documentation—that they had bought the land legitimately from Sutter. And those who purportedly purchased Sutter's land were locked in a prolonged general dispute with those who thought the land to be government property—free to whoever settled it first.

To be clear, Mexico granted Sutter nothing in Sacramento, despite a blizzard of contradictory maps and lawsuits stretching into the 1860s and reaching up to the U.S. Supreme Court. Sutter had conveniently lost the paperwork to support his claim. So the Settlers' Association went to Monterey and apparently brought back the truth that would spark an armed uprising.[14] The authentic document provided both a precise measurement of latitude and a clear physical description, which the Settlers duly translated and printed: Sutter's grant lay entirely between the Sacramento and Feather Rivers, which converge over ten miles to the north of town.[15]

But reality notwithstanding, the Supreme Court in 1864 drew an arbitrary line around a huge swath of land south of the American River. This declaration included Sutterville and part of Brighton and ironically followed the land grid later used to define property *not* included in Mexican grants. Supporting exhibits included a survey attributed to Jean Jacques Vioget that pasted wildly incorrect latitudes onto the Sacramento area. These readings not only belonged miles north of town but also were reversed—the larger measurement lay to the south! Any competent viewer would have realized

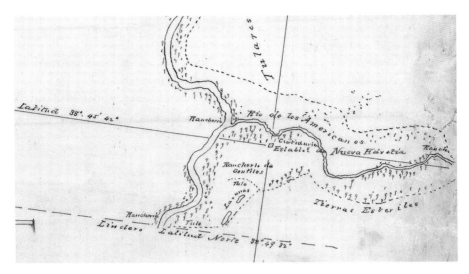

Jean Jacques Vioget's 1855 map of Sutter's claim accompanied a deposition by former Governor Juan Alvarado, despite egregious latitude errors. *Acc. 1980/132/0005, CSH.*

that these two measurements could not coexist anywhere in the northern hemisphere. This map was ridiculous, yet the Court accepted it as evidence for one of the period's most impactful land claim rulings.

Sacramento would have to live with Sutter's absurd claim, and that meant accepting a false history that was already a decade in the making. This revisionist narrative would obscure the role of Sacramento's elites in one of California's most dangerous and disturbing periods. Towns started vanishing around the time the Committees of Vigilance were conducting extralegal executions in the aftermath of Sacramento's settler uprising. This, too, has been forgotten. Sacramento's early days thus show how history can be rewritten to suit unscrupulous characters.

THE VIGILANTES

Stringing up villains is a brutally romantic part of Wild West lore. Such hangings are generally recalled as spontaneous outbreaks of collective violence. At times, remote communities were indeed outraged to the point of rash action when social order was sometimes weak or absent. But the Vigilance Committees were not a typical pioneer lynch mob. These were formal, durable organizations led by leading entrepreneurs of California's largest cities. They overthrew established law enforcement. They kept minutes.[16]

The San Francisco Vigilance Committees are somewhat well researched, even if most Californians are unfamiliar with their counterrevolutionary work. In *Dirty Deeds: Land, Violence and the 1856 San Francisco Vigilance Committee*, Nancy J. Taniguchi used long-hidden committee records to illustrate how this cabal of business leaders was driven by an insatiable thirst for land.[17] As in Sacramento, San Francisco real estate was tremendously valuable but plagued by serious title issues.

These committees were closely linked to Sacramento's ongoing squatter agitation. Order was supposedly restored after Sacramento City's 1850 unrest. But the reality is more complicated and much more disturbing. Although the Squatters' Riot was clearly suppressed, Sacramento remained contested space for months—Dr. Charles Robinson, a squatter leader, was elected to the first state assembly.[18] James McClatchy got into journalism, as the *Settlers and Miners Tribune* was issued from an office overlooking the intersection of 4th and J, where the riot's first shots were fired.[19] This was no mere gang of evicted squatters, fleeing the scene of the crime.

The Settlers' continued strength apparently triggered a brutal reaction, buried in Bancroft's 1888 *History of California*. Bancroft's primary narrative dismisses the entire settlers' movement, but a curious footnote stretching more than six pages tells the tale in rich detail. The first urban lynching of 1851 was reportedly triggered by "squatter trouble" in San Francisco.[20] However, the Vigilantes bagged their first kill in Sacramento City, where a gambler named Frederick Roe was hanged on February 25.

Although Eifler's book mostly concerns the Squatters' Riot, he incongruously includes a full chapter on the rise of lynch law, beginning with a conspicuous—and creepy—observation about one of Sacramento's most dramatic events. Residents departed from their usual practice of sharing details about their fascinating frontier lives in letters home as well as other channels. "The silence of that night remained nearly unbroken," he noted.[21] Only one account provided the basis for the sparse history of Roe's death: *Sacramento Transcript* editor F.C. Ewer initially sat on the mob's "jury" before he stepped back in the interest of supposedly disinterested reporting.[22]

But why did history fail to include the editorial perspective of the *Transcript*'s older rival, the *Placer Times*? For that matter, what happened to the *Times* editions published around the time of the Squatters' Riot? Despite that paper's absence from preserved collections, Sacramento's first history quotes its riot coverage at length, including a report that critics of the authorities' response had "prudently desisted."[23] In other words, they were silenced. And gaps in surviving newspapers paint a chilling picture.

Holes in the Story

Eifler must have been unaware of the *Daily Index*, whose largest surviving cache was tucked away at the New York Historical Society.[24] This paper reported explicit suppression of dissent as mob rule took hold. "Already have men ventured to declare that law is non-existent," it warned, "while others have not scrupled to threaten the denouncers of yesterday's proceedings, with a like visitation of the vengeance of the public will."[25]

The *Index*'s disappearance was not simply an isolated failure to archive the issues of a single publication. *Hundreds* of issues of several key local newspapers are missing from accessible collections. The gaps interrupt both of Sacramento City's first newspapers at critical times. At least one journalist, the *Times*' J.E. Lawrence, was brutally assaulted and threatened with death over something printed in one of these missing editions.

Disaster would be one plausible reason for missing newspapers— Sacramento City was flammable as well as flood-prone. But in such an accident, all issues prior to the proposed disaster would probably be lost. Most of the city's papers would exhibit roughly simultaneous ends to their gaps. These gaps would correspond to actual disasters, and the first issues surviving after a gap would be filled with accounts of recovery. But no such signatures of disaster appear. Instead, gaps in preserved collections vary by publication and cluster around moments of high conflict. This points toward intentional removal of issues because of unacceptable editorial content—such as the *Times*' post-riot report that the opposition was being silenced, or whatever provoked Lawrence's assailants amid the Vigilantes' rising reign of terror.

The California Digital Newspaper Collection (CDNC) is the state's most comprehensive and accessible aggregation of early newspapers. It includes most specimens held by major California research institutions. Although not entirely exhaustive, this searchable online collection provides reasonably complete access to newspapers that were successfully archived. It is a useful measure of what has been available to historians over time.

A brief overview of the gaps illustrates their suspicious nature. The CDNC holds all copies of the *Placer Times*' first year, from its 1849 launch until June 7, 1850—about two months before the Squatters' Riot and one month before Norristown suddenly vanished from the news. Surviving issues of the *Sacramento Transcript*, which is the only available local newspaper after the *Times* vanished, run from its April 1850 debut until June 5, 1851. The *Transcript* and *Times* were combined shortly thereafter, on June 16. But the final editions of each independent paper are gone, along with issues published after the merger and before the combined paper's odd move to San Francisco one year later. The intercity wave of media consolidation eventually rolled the *Placer Times*, the *Transcript* and the *Alta California* into a single San Francisco paper by 1855—incidentally just in time for the 1856 Committees of Vigilance. The *Daily Union* seems to be the only Sacramento paper with an uninterrupted and accessible collection past mid-1851.[26] As we shall see, that paper's reporting is suspect.

That June was an especially momentous month in California vigilantism, and reports from San Francisco suggests that something was seriously amiss. On the eighth, three days after the *Transcript*'s disappearance, San Francisco's *Alta* published a call for a "war of extermination" against Australians—popular scapegoats at that time.[27] On the ninth, the San Francisco Committee of Vigilance was organized in a warehouse belonging to Sam Brannan, institutionalizing mob rule. The next day, an Australian was hanged by a huge mob in San Francisco's first successful lynching. This was an unfortunate week to have lost Sacramento's most experienced editorial viewpoints.[28]

Indeed the *Alta* ominously reported, "A Vigilance Committee of 213 signers has been found in Sacramento....The Sacramento papers contain very litte [sic] news."[29] So where were the newspapers? Did the *Times* and the *Transcript* each simply take some time off, perhaps to go panning for gold? There is no evidence of such interruptions. Each paper is mentioned by the other during archival gaps, confirming ongoing publication. The *Transcript*'s report of the April 1851 assault on *Times* editor James E. Lawrence is only the most alarming such example.[30]

Historians have generally ignored the Lawrence incident and also missed the community's vigorous response. A rare and surprising exception is the 1880 account by Thomas Thompson and Albert West in their *History of Sacramento County California*. They noted that "threats were openly made by the rough element that they would treat the next editor that ventured to intervene with them, in a worse manner." This assault on the press reportedly prompted an "address" signed by more than one thousand people. This statement of public sentiment described and condemned a more generalized threat to journalism.[31] The controversy's conclusion remains unknown, left unmentioned in the city's emerging historic narrative.

In 1853, the *Union*'s publisher, John Morse, produced *History of Sacramento*, which compounded the archival gaps' damage by simply avoiding the vividly memorable events of two years prior. One might hope that a newspaper publisher would give an accurate account, but instead Morse did grave damage to Sacramento's collective memory with obviously intentional disinformation. He did offer detailed reporting of the land controversies that plagued Sacramento in 1850, including the Squatters' Riot. His account is fairly even-handed up to the great clash and includes excerpts from numerous primary sources, as well as his own interpretation. It is nicely done.

But when Morse reaches the Squatters' Riot, he suddenly relies on previously published accounts instead of original analysis. And to avoid mentioning the Vigilance Committees, he provides an absurdly inaccurate summary of 1851: "The winter passed away almost unnoticed, save by its genial influences, and never were realized more delightful comminglings of business and pleasure." Then, in a bizarre shift of style, events of that dark spring are reduced to a disjointed list of notes from his newspaper's files. His first such entry is dated in April, weeks after Rowe's lynching and the same month that Lawrence was brutalized: "Green peas in market."[32]

Despite its severe flaws, Morse's account was enshrined as Sacramento's first history. As a result, the city's historiography has been built on omissions and falsehood. This troublesome foundation was returned to prominence in 1997, when the California State Library Foundation reprinted his mangled account as a companion to a reproduction of the 1853–54 city directory. Despite severe shortcomings, Morse's history is evidently the oldest to survive a plague of revisionism. It is valuable as a journalist's account, written only a few years after the fact. To his credit, Morse captures a lost news report that reveals clear suppression of dissent following one of Sacramento's most traumatic incidents—an important clue about when that source disappeared. But Morse's value is not in his recall of facts as they happened. Rather, he illuminates clear breaks in the historic narrative. He shows what can happen when a community cannot bear to look at its past.

If someone wanted to lose a town—or several—this would be a golden opportunity.

The 1850s were a period of great turmoil in Sacramento, marred by significant holes in the historic record and coinciding with violent unrest as well as documented attacks on dissent. But none of this proves the extraordinary charge of civic cannibalism. The demise of Lost Sacramentos may not be directly related to those years of conflict in and around Sacramento City. The direct connections between the Committees of Vigilance and journalistic gaps remain similarly murky. Only a major research initiative will confirm how, or whether, Sacramento City actually ate its neighbors. But the sole survivor's account is highly suspect in such cases. So an inquiry should begin by identifying what parties have gone missing.

CHAPTER 2

SUTTERVILLE

By James C. Scott

Sacramento's William Land Park is a living heirloom. Brought to life through the largess of a wealthy hotelier and the earnest efforts of early city reformers, the space has passed between generations as a refuge from the demands of urban life. Few would know, though, that its southernmost entry point—at what today is the five-pointed intersection of Sutterville Road, Del Rio Road and South Land Park Drive—occupies a spot that would have been a couple blocks from the north edge of the now extinct village of Sutterville, a place whose foundation precedes Sacramento's by several months, if not years. Despite that, Sutterville was quickly consumed by the fogs of history, while its northern neighbor endured, becoming inland California's largest and most consequential city. At the heart of understanding this puzzling dynamic is the following question: How could Sutterville, a location with nearly every natural advantage suitable to successful cityhood, be supplanted by Sacramento City, a spot with comparatively few?

First envisioned by Johann Sutter during the winter months of 1844–45, the two-hundred-lot town was to be located, according to longtime Sutter clerk Heinrich Lienhard, "four miles southwest of [Sutter's] fort on high ground near a deep lagoon a mile back from the Sacramento River, a location considered safe from floods."[33] The spot's elevation and relative security from the seasonable flooding that Sutter had grown all too familiar with since 1839 were *the* primary considerations in the town ending up where, in his words, "the banks of the river [didn't] overflow."[34] Called Montezuma until June 1847, Suttersville as late as April 1848 and then a less parochial-sounding (or so it was believed at the time) Sutter for some period after, the spot's more familiar name, Sutterville, took on permanent use just prior to the American Civil War.

Platting for Sutterville began in early 1846 as Sutter lieutenants John Bidwell and Lansford Hastings spent just over a week laying out the initial grid.[35] The spot's geographic appeal is clearly seen in a 1907 USGS topographical map, with a rise in elevation appearing a half mile inward from the Sacramento

River. If we use the 1853 Vance Building (today memorialized by an "E Clampus Vitus" plaque on the south side of Sutterville Road) as our point of orientation, Sutterville was roughly half as far from the river as Lienhard would lead us to believe. And through a modern lens, the bottom of the "deep lagoon" at ten feet above sea level would have most certainly been at what is now the low-lying South Land Park Terrace Tract, a difference of nearly nineteen feet from where one stands at the Vance Building pylon (thirty feet above sea level). It's likely the lake's remnants make up what's left of the Sacramento Drainage Canal, constructed in the 1870s to aid with flood abatement. Stretching from 6th and R Streets to Sutterville and points south, the canal is now a north–south arrangement of lakelets that dot the landscape like so many random pearls on a string, offering a faint sense of the water feature that, as we'll see, proved such a millstone to early Suttervillians.

Various other factors seem to have influenced Sutterville's birth. By the mid-1840s, the pleasing solitude that Sutter had grown so accustomed to since first arriving in the Sacramento Valley was ebbing away. Some sources indicate that the new town was to be a release valve for Sutter—a way to alleviate his fort of the growing number of settlers landing in and around its walls who, according to historian James P. Zollinger, were making Sutter "sick and tired."[36] As Sutter wrote in December 1844, "The people are becoming daring due to strong immigration; just now a very

Opposite: Part of a 1907 USGS map shows the rough location of Sutterville and an increase in elevation as one moves farther east from the Sacramento River. *USGS.*

Above: This 1927 aerial shows where most of Sutterville sat. Sutterville Road and the Southern Pacific line intersect near the city's northernmost and last standing structure, the Vance Building. Visible are remnants of the lagoon—the drainage canal and a pond. *UCSB.*

strong party has arrived with eleven wagons and ten families."[37] Just over a year later, Sutter welcomed the birth of Sutterville as "a great relief for the Establishment [*sic*] here, when I think I will have a little easy time, other arrivals are coming, which interfere very often too much with my business…the new city…a distance of about 5 miles from here, will make my establishment more agreeable."[38]

Beyond a way to recolonize the unwanted, historian Mark Eifler posits that Sutter saw the new town as a viable diplomatic and commercial linchpin between the burgeoning American settlements at, and above, the confluence of the Sacramento and American Rivers and the Mexican outpost at Yerba Buena, renamed San Francisco in 1847.[39] Sutter, speaking in reference to Sutterville on May 12, 1848, had enough interest and hope in the town's standing to crow that it would "soon be next in size to San Francisco among California towns."[40] Certainly, if there were to be an inland metropolis in California and counterweight to coastal San Francisco, Sutter wanted to be at the front end of its foundation. Historian Donald Pisani asserts that Sutter, prior to the Mexican-American War, even envisioned Sutterville as a successor to Monterey as the capital of Alta California.[41] Mexico's defeat changed all of that, but we also know that, as early as spring 1845, Sutter was pragmatic enough to consider what life could look like in a post–Mexican Alta California, viewing the region in a possible "union with Oregon" where "a great and powerful 'Pacific Republic' might be created, with the most magnificent prospects," and one that "within a few years [would] gain strength for a complete declaration of its independence."[42] It's hardly a stretch, then, that Sutter may have seen Sutterville as a viable administrative center of a new nation state.

The town also looks to have been founded on the promise of agricultural commerce—a riverside gateway through which the yield of the Sacramento Valley's rich alluvial soil could transit for sale along the Sacramento River and points beyond. Sutter seems to have obsessed about the role of agriculture in the economic growth of Alta California, touting New Helvetia's "excellent water communications" and "facilities unsurpassed in the world."[43] Settlers quickly learned that the soil in (and for leagues in any direction around) Sutterville—a combination of Columbia and San Joaquin silt loams— was prime for agricultural development.[44] In 1850, one Sutterville farmer named M. Wells advertised the sale of an astonishing ten thousand pounds of produce, including squash, pumpkins, corn and potatoes.[45] Pennsylvania-born John S. Harbinson then followed, establishing by the mid-1850s one of the Sacramento Valley's first nurseries of fruit and shade trees and quickly making Sutterville a seeding hub for orchards throughout the Sacramento River Delta and American River watershed.[46] It was also in Sutterville that Harbison established one of Northern California's largest apiaries.[47] The geographical positioning of the town, essentially halfway between the heart of the Sacramento Valley and the Golden Gate, is also notable. The settlement sat at or very near the so-called head of navigation, a spot providing the ideal balance of proximity to products—in this case agriculture—and convenient access to deep-river and ocean trade routes, offering ready access to markets around the vast San Francisco Bay and up and down the California coastline and beyond.[48] To Sutter, this meant as far north as Alaska and as far west as Tahiti.[49]

A less explored consideration in Sutterville's birth relates to the Germanic Swiss Sutter growing up in the shadow of a pre-industrial Holy Roman Empire, a mosh of absolutist, quasi-independent states, many with their own language, monetary unit and system of weights and measures, with almost

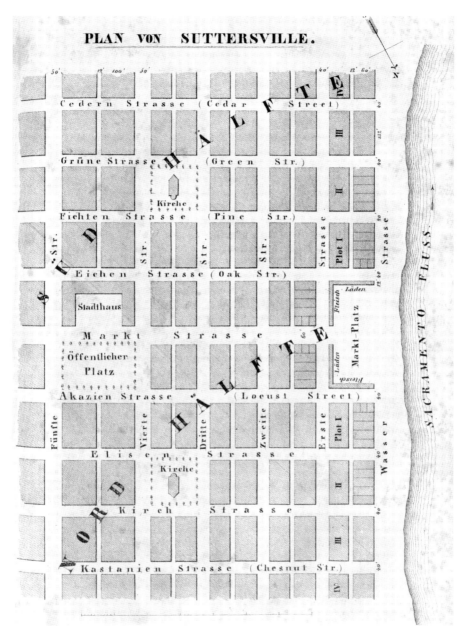

Schmolder's map of a would-be Suttersville is reminiscent of a nineteenth-century European agricapital. *SPL.*

all relying on agriculture as their primary industry. This is what Sutter knew, and there's ample reason to pose the possibility that the new town, in his eyes, would be to New Helvetia as Stuttgart was to Baden-Wurttemberg or Munich to Bavaria, riverside capitals that, while member to a loosely bound political arrangement, were free to seek their own wealth and maintain their own independence—two things greatly valued by Sutter. Even an 1847 map created by Sutter associate Captain Bruno Schmolder possesses the planning and charm of an Old World–style capital with Stadthaus, public square and riverfront marketplace prominently displayed—a fitting centerpiece to Sutter's so-called Pazifische Republik.[50]

From birth, Sutterville possessed the types of institutions one would expect to find in a growing city. In 1847, it became home to the area's first brick structure, built by talented Alsatian George Zins, who went on to establish a brickyard in Sutterville, large enough to produce 100,000 bricks in 1848.[51] Zins's building was described by traveler Theodore T. Johnson as "some two or three hundred yards back" from the riverbank, where "the country still rises more, and here, on a beautiful green bank, is a substantial and neat brick house, constructed of brick, a kiln of which is near at hand."[52] From a city building standpoint, Zins's business is remarkable, for it is arguably the Sacramento area's first industrial endeavor. It's also noteworthy that Sutter envisioned this very possibility as early as January 1846, when he stated, "There in front of the Hills between them is a small lake which will be of great service for Atobe's [sic], and then afterwards can easily be filled up."[53] Its series of brick structures set Sutterville apart from Sacramento City in these early years, which, when considered in context, is meaningful. While Sacramento City was losing 70 percent of its buildings (most composed of wood) in the great fire of November 1852 and was awash in the inundation of early 1853, Sutterville sat protected from flood by its elevation and was somewhat aloof from flame by the "fire-proof wood" of the day, brick.

Further signs of cityhood soon followed. The Columbia Hotel, regarded to be the first public structure in what became Sacramento County, was in business by midsummer 1848. Meanwhile, Sutter celebrated "a great many German mechanics" building houses in the fall of 1847. A school was being planned for late 1847, and a ferry offering access to both banks of the Sacramento River was also in the works.[54] We're also told in Sutter's *New Helvetia Diary* that, in April 1848, he sent "some sick boys [to] Sutterville for the Doctor," who may have been Ohio-born "Physician and Surgeon" T.M. Ames; by 1849, a law office had also been established.[55] At around this time, an anonymous miner described Sutterville to be "all…

Shown is an initialed brick created at George Zins's Sutterville brickyard. The Alsatian Zins was also a noted brewmaster. *CSP*.

bustle and activity….[with] an [*sic*] hotel, stores with dry goods, a distillery, a blacksmith's and wheelwright's."[56] Johnson also went on to claim that "[Sutter had] all the advantages of [Sacramento City]…besides high grounds a quarter of a mile back from the river, it must soon gain upon its rival in permanent in population."[57]

There was clearly ample optimism for Sutterville's future. Yet sitting between the town (resting generally on a north–south highland) and the Sacramento River was the lagoon that stretched roughly a half mile parallel to the river.[58] Despite the water feature's looming presence, all surveys of the town placed parcels inside of it, implying that both draining and filling were inevitable, with Sutter believing that it could "easely [*sic*] be filled up."[59] What appears to be the only effort to deal with the lagoon came in the spring of 1849, as businessman George McDougal, having just moved to Sutterville from Sacramento City, paid two men the obscene sum of $3,500 to "make a road through the lake," which amounted to more of a causeway.[60] But even with the new viaduct, port facilities were considered inadequate and narrow, wedged into limited space between the river and the lagoon.[61] Lieutenant George H. Derby, topographical engineer for an 1849 U.S. Army expedition to the newly opened gold fields, stated that "the portion of the 'city' on the river [ostensibly the port] is a horrible sand bank infested with ravenous tribes of mosquitoes; immediately in rear of which is a swamp…beyond

VIEW

This 1855 rendering shows a panorama of Sutterville as viewed from the bank of the Sacramento. Visible is the lagoon and viaduct. *SPL.*

the swamp it extends into a plain where I believe it is not possible to live."[62] Derby's description of the village paints a bleak picture, but perhaps more notably, he fingers the albatross that both the lagoon and Sutterville's poor harbor facilities had truly become.

So, to what factors can we attribute the demise of Sutterville? Capitalism may be the easiest and best answer. Beyond that, the meddling of business savant Sam Brannan, an absent and indebted Sutter Sr., a naïve and malaria-stricken Johann Augustus Sutter Jr., the insidious reach of a pro–Sacramento City newspaper, a lagoon problem, a harbor problem and luck must all be considered.

By late 1848, the elder Sutter's debt had reached a high tide, accented by a whopping $30,000 owed to the Russian-American Fur Company. When Sutter Jr. arrived in California, he was welcomed by a degraded fort and a

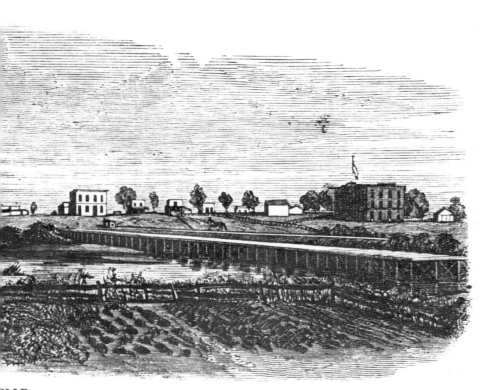

ILLE.

father who was unfit to do much at all, leaving the son to, in effect, make everything go away. The young Swiss must have been staggered by what was asked of him. Panicked to settle his father's open accounts, he was easily convinced by Brannan to sell lots in the low floodplains that occupied the heart of Sacramento City—$500 per lot near the embarcadero and $250 per lot closer to the fort. With such dizzying debt on the Sutter name, Brannan also made the point that since Senior owned so little of Sutterville after having sold or gifted most lots away—with most held by McDougal—there was clearly more money to be made by selling those in Sacramento City that Sutter actually owned. Once Junior had done so, there was no turning back. Moving forward, nearly all the capital in the region was funneled into a town that would flood within the next year—and five more times between 1850 and 1863.

Sutterville had clear advantages over Sacramento City, but it didn't have Brannan. Smart, without scruples, a gambler of anything and everything and willing to use violence to get his way, the native Mainer had established a commercial presence along the upstream embarcadero at Front and J Streets by early 1849. And he wasn't alone in doing so. Names like Blackburn, Hensley, Reading, Priest and Lee planted their flags along Front and 2nd Streets, seizing what Eifler called the "geography of trade."[63] The wide and accessible wharf at Sacramento City offered easy access to supplies and quick succor for thousands of eager miners, while accommodating a quickly growing business class that sold its wares out of everything from boats to tents to rickety wood-frame structures. *Placer Times* editor Edward Kemble described a riverfront of "twenty-five or thirty stores…together with a hotel, printing office, bakery, blacksmith shops, tin shop, billiard room, bowling alley, etc. each indispensable in making up the vast compound of a city. Sacramento City is probably as healthy a locality as this valley affords."[64] And that—even before Sutterville had any physical connectivity from town to riverbank—was what the miner, merchant and anyone with any interest in benefiting from the gold rush was reading in the area's only newspaper of record, one that was arguably partial to Brannan and the town's other founders. The mere presence of a newspaper gave the frontier city considerable cachet. It could also act as a broadcaster and booster of the merits of its town over that of rivals, a fact that Sutter was savvy to as early as 1846.[65] In this respect, the truth was what the *Placer Times* said it was, and there was very little that it had to say about Sutterville, a spot without any paper to champion its cause. Although not in direct reference to Brannan's deliberate alienation of Sutterville, John Plumbe, photographer and witness to much on the ground in 1849, saw Kemble as a stooge of the northerly city's merchant and speculator class, willingly "servile [with his] mercenary readiness to please his wealthy patrons—forgetting that *truth* is one of the most indispensable attributes of a gentleman."[66]

Sutterville merchants explored myriad ways to lure Sacramento City's business owners and miners south: selling goods at cost, attempting to bolster port facilities and enticing relocation by the gifting of parcels. But none of that worked. And while Sutter and the Suttervillians failed miserably at leveraging geography to their advantage, Brannan could shape it to his, doing so by further turning Junior's attention away from Sutterville by pointing to the labor costs attached to fording, draining and filling the lagoon, or what early Sacramento City historian John Frederick Morse referred to as the "slough of despondency."[67] Sacramento City's embarcadero, on the other hand, required no such investment. In the words of historian Ernest Lehr, "Sutterville's poor harbor was a greater disadvantage than elevated land secure from floods when there were no floods."[68] And there would be no

Shown is a depiction of an active harborside at Sutterville, circa 1850. *SPL.*

floods until early 1850, by which time Sacramento City had furthered its civic primacy and Brannan had become one of the wealthiest men in the American West.

Yet even after Sacramento City achieved cityhood, there were signs that Sutterville still possessed ambitions. In July 1849, traveler J.M. Letts revealed that upon going ashore, he "had the pleasure of making the acquaintance of one of the proprietors, with whom we walked a mile back from the town to view 'Capitol Hill,' the anticipated site of the State House."[69] While impossible to prove, a simple drive down South Land Park Drive, southward from its intersection with Sutterville Road, may indicate the location of the would-be capitol building. Positioned at the intersection of Ridgeway Drive and South Land Park Drive and at a crest of thirty-nine feet above sea level, we see the highest point in South Land Park Terrace and one of the highest elevations in all of Sacramento proper.

Talk of a would-be Capitol Hill is not the talk of a defeated resident in a defeated town. Attorney William Muldrow followed with the purchase of a brick hotel and various other structures in the summer of 1854, hoping to establish a college at Sutterville. From spots as far away as Oroville in the north and Sonoma to the west, African Americans in the summer of 1860 convened in Sutterville to picnic and listen to speeches to honor the emancipation of the enslaved peoples of the West Indies. We also know that the so-called Dr. Lola, a Chinese-born herbalist, ran a small business out a brick structure in Sutterville as early as 1857. And filing for incorporation with the State of California in February 1863, but never built, was the Sutterville Railroad, which was to run from the river city and intersect with the Sacramento Valley Railroad (SVRR) to the east. Albeit a mere three miles in length, the line provides proof of someone's vision of Sutterville as a point of transit for goods delivered by water and then pushed on by rail, and vice versa. Without surprise, the timing coincides with the Great Flood of 1861–62, which had brought so much devastation to Sacramento City, including the SVRR's R Street depot.

Just years into incorporation, Sacramento City had been faced with saving itself from fire, flood and disease. After the inundation of 1852–53, Sacramento City publishers Edmund Barber and George Baker breathlessly admired the city's repeated attempts to survive through civic and commercial engagement, saying that so much public confidence in the endeavor existed that "[Sacramento City's] aspiring neighbors at Sutterville relaxed their energies, seeing how hopeless was the chase, and Sutterville remained as she remains to-day—a 'deserted village,' and an object of inquiry to the traveler, who beholds its solitary mansions, as he passes by, bound on his way amid the broad windings of the Sacramento."[70] And with a dash of schadenfreude, the *Sacramento Bee* said of a sleepy Sutterville in February 1857:

> *We found a number of comparatively new but abandoned and desolate brick buildings, standing here and there in "solitary grandeur" on the site of what was expected to be that mighty city of the occident. There stood a gigantic mercantile building, full of emptiness…the winds like spirits, whispered in its walls…yonder stood a meat market, which we approached, but found neither mutton, pork nor beef—not even the ghost of a butcher was visible.*[71]

As late as the great flood of 1861–62, though, the editors of the *Nevada Democrat* criticized Sacramento City founders for "building the city upon a site known to be subject to terrible overflows, when they might have built upon high ground at Sutterville."[72] But none of that would matter. By 1863, the central business district of Sacramento City had been raised by several feet, a river had been diverted with the intent to ease flooding and any geographic advantage that Sutterville possessed had been rendered moot.

Sutterville's competition with Sacramento City proved all too common a sight in the American West. Portland had Oregon City, St. Helens, St. Johns and Milwaukie to grapple with; Seattle had Everett and Tacoma; Kansas

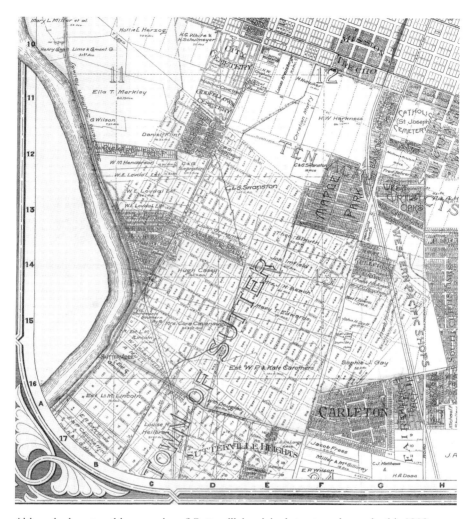

Although almost nothing remains of Sutterville's original streets and parcels, this 1913 map by Phinney, Cate & Marshall superimposes the old grid on modern Land Park. *CSH.*

City had Leavenworth and Atchison; and Chicago had Waukegan. The frontier proved a veritable Ouija board whereby Adam Smith's "invisible hand" guided the fates of individuals, businesses and embryo cities alike. What's more, early town platting and boosting meshed with the West's gambling culture, often driven—like a miner in search of gold or a monte player awaiting their next card—by the ardent belief that a certain harbor or riverfront would become the next New York City, as aptly reflected by Colonel Jonathan D. Stevenson's 1849 founding of the optimistically named

New York of the Pacific, located at the mouth of Sacramento and San Joaquin Rivers. Like Sutterville, Stevenson's town possessed several features favorable to sustained growth, but it, too, foundered in the face of rivals.

While several factors affected Sutterville's limited development, William Tecumseh Sherman, who surveyed large sections of land in Northern California both before and just after the start of the gold rush and knew Sutterville along with Stevenson's New York of the Pacific, offered the simplest and perhaps most plausible of them all (emphasis added):

> *At Sutterville, the plateau of the Sacramento approached quite near the river, and it would have been a better site for a town than the low, submerged land where the city now stands; but it seems to be a law of growth that all natural advantages are disregarded wherever once business chooses a location. Old Sutter's embarcadero became Sacramento City, simply because it was the first point used for unloading boats for Sutter's Fort, just as the site for San Francisco was fixed by the use of Yerba Buena as the hide landing for the Mission of "San Francisco de Asis."[73]*

Today, the spot once occupied by Sutterville's brick buildings is covered with residential subdivisions, a midcentury-era shopping mall and a band of Interstate 5 running over the general location of the would-be city's primeval lagoon and harbor. So quickly had Sutterville fallen that by 1858, it was shortlisted as a possible home to a new state prison. Instead of pressing brick along the Sacramento, however, prisoners ended up harvesting granite along the American near Folsom.[74] Without incorporation or becoming a penal colony, Sutterville kept its rural identity for nearly a century more as dairies and other agricultural endeavors, primarily fruit orchards, were operated by people with names like Rocca, Lopez, Bagwell and Goodrich. The Vance Building, which became Martin Arenz's Sutterville Brewery and then a jazz and country club well into the late 1930s, was the last of Sutterville's original structures, razed in the mid-1950s out of concern for public safety. The race- and class-exclusive South Land Park Terrace then followed, promoting itself in the late 1940s as a "highly restrictive…future homesite" on a "Historic Landsite."[75] Today's only visible nods to Sutterville are an elementary school and a road that starts at one freeway and ends at another, providing a tepid epitaph for a place that could have been a modern port city, the capital city of California or the jewel of a Pacific Rim nation-state.

CHAPTER 3

BRIGHTON

By Andrew McLeod

In May 1850, Captain Roland Gelston set sail up the American River. His schooner *Curlew* carried 162 tons of freight—including six houses.[76] This massive cargo was bound for Brighton, about eight miles upstream. Gelston's bold shipment displayed great optimism about the new town—at least among its promoters. And confidence spread quickly. Soon, Warbass & Company began advertising its role as Brighton's primary real estate vendor; at least one big player in the region's tumultuous real estate market was betting on "one of the most eligible and healthy resorts that can be found in the valley of Sacramento."[77] This notice was still running in August when it appeared—rather awkwardly—in the same issue of the *Transcript* that reported the "Squatters' Riot" death of Sheriff Joseph McKinney.[78] After the first battle in Sacramento City, McKinney was determined to root out any remaining members of the Settlers' Association. He had intelligence that "squatters" were regrouping in Brighton, so he gathered a posse and rode east into an ambush that remains the mostly forgotten town's best-recalled event.

Brighton apparently remained a stronghold of Settler resistance for years, while its landownership was hotly contested. But before the summer's violence and residual turmoil, Brighton was open for business. This excellent location offered attractive properties at a major crossroads on a high southern bank overlooking a wide stretch of river with a relatively slow current. It was also miles closer to the mines than Sacramento City, an attractive stop for thirsty and gold-laden miners. A nearby ford crossed the river to the Nisenan village of Kadema, and another route headed south across low grassy hills. Brighton was a splendid place to settle or speculate. And while its name remains vaguely and faintly attached to the vicinity, nothing remains of the original waterfront junction.

Historians blame its disappearance, vaguely, on title trouble.

We should not be surprised at rival claims for this plum property, as Gelston and Warbass were hardly the first to notice the value of Brighton's land. Johann Sutter himself attempted to construct a flour mill here in 1847 but had to abandon the project when his Mormon workers left for the Mother Lode the next year.[79] It is unclear why Sutter did not simply pivot to the Indigenous labor that he habitually exploited. In any case, Brighton's geography offered an obvious place to settle. But then that settlement mysteriously stopped. Brighton was cleared out, and it remained mostly empty for more than a century. Whoever legally owned the land under Brighton, its valuable waterfront never developed in a way that left any durable mark.

Brighton certainly faced adverse claims of landownership; such disputes were widespread if not universal around Gold Rush California. But "title trouble" is a superficial description of what likely occurred at Brighton. The town was apparently a geographic and political nexus of a profound conflict that apparently challenged Sacramento City's fundamental system of real estate ownership, as well as the purported value of Manifest Destiny's distribution of land into the "right" hands.

Even if the underlying land wasn't the legal property of Gelston and company, *someone* owned this prime real estate. Why wouldn't the eventual victor in any land contest have maintained the existing streets and parcels, which would have held more value than undivided land littered with traces of prior occupation? Why wouldn't a settlement here do at least as well as Folsom, for instance? Why wouldn't at least a few of Brighton's structures have survived, with whoever had built on properties willing to grit their teeth and buy the land under their improvements a second time? Unfortunately, the documents most useful for reconstructing who lived in Brighton—and when and why they left—are gone.

Historians have generally avoided Brighton. Most of the historiography regarding its origination and development merely rehashes the same simple story—usually beginning with something like the account given in Thompson & West's 1880 *History of Sacramento County, California*: "The Town of Brighton was started in 1849 by a party of Sacramento speculators including Gelston;

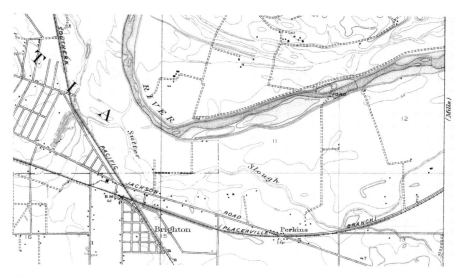

This 1911 map shows Brighton's waterfront emptied out despite the attraction of a nearby ford, with development clustered along California's oldest rail line. *USGS.*

The 1928 aerial photograph shows rectangular fields, possibly derived from Brighton's street grid, as well as standing water in Sutter's Slough from recent flooding. *UCSB.*

the town plot was made, lots staked off, a race track, and the Pavilion Hotel, built by the originators of the enterprise." Brighton was, at least briefly, "a lively place."[80]

Brighton seemed lively enough during the summer of 1850, when the new community hosted a Fourth of July celebration that attracted prominent area citizens to the Pavilion, a grand three-story hotel. Thirty guns were fired at Sacramento City, corresponding with the number of the states. These reports were answered by another thirty at Brighton and the same number at Washington (now West Sacramento). After the racket died down, Brighton heard from two big players in Sacramento City land speculation: George McKinstry, Esq., read the Declaration of Independence, and Colonel E.J.C. Kewen gave an oration.[81]

Brighton clearly had potential, even if investments there ultimately didn't pan out. And despite later claims of abandonment, Brighton was reportedly home to passionate and organized settlers through at least the 1850s. Brighton's demise was deeply entangled with the region's troubled history of land speculation and "squatter trouble." But despite its memorable historic events, Brighton's location, physical composition and disappearance remain mostly unexplored puzzles of Sacramento's history.

Where Was Brighton?

Four places have shared the name Brighton. First came the original gold rush riverfront near modern Howe Avenue. The second Brighton was a railroad town established in 1855, later renamed Perkins; this still stands as a more typical historic town remnant, enveloped by suburbia. The third was Brighton Junction, located where Sacramento's first two railroads crossed near modern Folsom Boulevard and 65th Street. All three were apparently located within the original footprint of the 1850 survey, which is discussed soon. Finally, Brighton Township was one of fourteen county divisions created in 1852; this encompassed a large area south of the river, stretching five miles south to the town of Florin and nine miles east to west.

The original Brighton was home to one of the Sacramento region's initial attempts at durable settler infrastructure, a flour mill launched by the man with the region's earliest European claim to the land (however false it may have been). A gristmill would have been a key part of Sutter's erstwhile empire. It was never operational, but construction progressed to the point that there was building enough for Sam Brannan to purchase, move and redeploy as the City Hotel downstream.[82] Yet the closest recognition of the mill attempt is Gristmill Recreation Area, which marks the ditch's intake several miles upstream.

The mill survived on paper for years after its builders departed for the golden hills. The 1851 Brighton plat map still identified a reserve for a mill, as well as a diagonal millrace to provide water. This canal reserve cut through nearly twenty well-located urban parcels. Maps do not equal reality, but even the potential for a canal complicated these parcels' use while also offering a lucrative resource—water would boost land values through irrigation, as well as potential power for turning millstones. Alas, the mill never came. Neither did the water.

But Brighton already had plenty of water. Its best amenity was the river itself, which required no construction. Downstream, the channel provided access in its natural state, and the landing itself faced a long stretch of broad, slow and deep water. Gelston's bulk delivery shows that large craft could reach Brighton, at least during the late spring after floods subsided but before the channel became too shallow with the dry season. The California legislature declared the American River navigable to Brighton in 1851.[83]

Brighton was also a key junction for roads to the gold—the greatest attractant to settlers and the greatest single driver of development at that

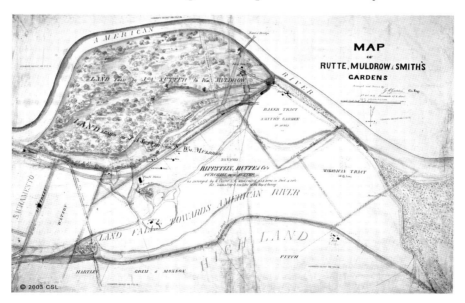

G.H. Goddard's 1857 *Map of Rutte, Muldrow & Smith's Gardens* shows roads and crossings along modern Elvas Boulevard. A trail continues upstream toward Brighton. *CSL.*

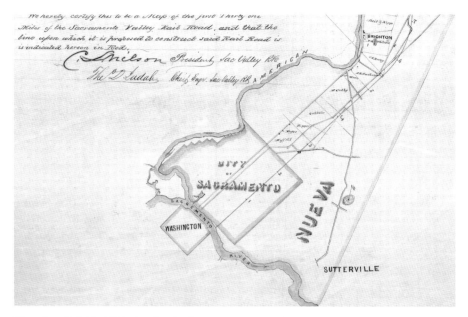

Theodore Judah's 1854 plan for the Sacramento Valley Railroad captured Brighton's remaining features as well as the Sutterville-Brighton Road. *CSA.*

time. The town stood at a natural chokepoint along one of the nineteenth-century world's most dynamic land corridors. At least three major routes converged here: The J Street road provided a straight shot from Sacramento City to the Brighton waterfront. A river road connected to Sacramento City's northern waterfronts as late as 1857 (discussed in the next chapter). The Sutterville-Brighton Road, which bypassed the Sacramento City bottomlands, was important enough for the county to designate J.H. Stewart supervisor in 1854.[84]

But it wasn't just wagons rolling into Brighton. Years before Theodore Judah's transcontinental line transformed Sacramento, his first California rails breathed new life into a struggling town. The Sacramento Valley Railroad would include a station here, and Judah's 1854 plan is the best surviving depiction of the general location; it clearly places Brighton south of the river, just upstream of the northward curve that takes the river past what is today the university and toward Cal Expo. Judah shows a cluster of riverside buildings as well as a racetrack, confirming that the waterfront and the Sutterville-Brighton Road survived until at least the mid-1850s.

After that, Brighton disappeared.

Government Land

Locating Brighton should be a simple matter of consulting the county assessor's map books, which serve as a key record of landownership and tax receipts. Every year or two, parcel boundaries were clearly if imprecisely delineated in these books; subdivisions were also depicted in detail on their own pages. Alas, the oldest year held by the Center for Sacramento History dates from 1870, omitting the county's first two decades. There is apparently no visual record of Sacramento County landownership for the years in which Brighton rose and fell. It is unclear whether those map books were destroyed, lost, hidden or simply never created. In any case, identifying earlier landowners requires a laborious search at the county recorder's office, through deeds that are often written in verbose and ornate handwriting that defies comprehension. Even worse, the oldest available assessor map is grievously inaccurate, moving the rails and river toward each other and squeezing Brighton by about half.[85] Small wonder there was some trouble tracking ownership.

Judah's railroad map remains the best depiction of Brighton's original location. But unfortunately this map was on a regional scale and made no effort to mark any surviving boundaries to show Brighton's original extent. It attempted only to show Brighton as a location along the proposed route rather than locate individual features within that location. Still, it confirms Brighton's general location and approximate layout of at least nine buildings and three streets between the racecourse and the river.

Luckily, Brighton may be located using another county record. *Subdivision Map Book 1* is a grab bag from Sacramento County's early years, the first volume of an ongoing series that preserves whatever maps were submitted to the public record.[86] A detailed 1850 plat of Brighton is the fourth document in this compilation—one of the first maps ever preserved outside Sacramento City. Although this record does not establish the county's endorsement of Brighton's legitimacy, it does suggest some recognition of the landownership underlying the town. Whatever questions were later raised about Brighton titles, the county recorder received this map precisely depicting it. Recorded in January 1851, this remarkable document provides the exact dimensions of Brighton, if not its location. This plat reveals the speculative vision of what could have been—thousands of people, probably hundreds of businesses and, of course, a racetrack and mill. Brighton would cover nearly a square mile.

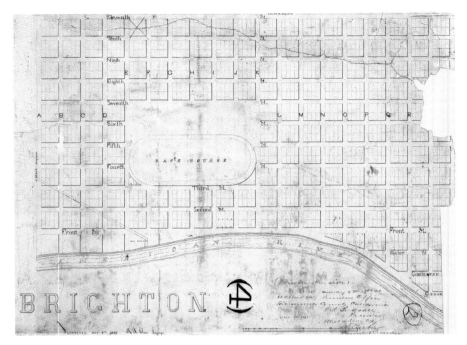

This plat of Brighton was surveyed in 1850 and recorded with the county in 1851. The viewer faces southward, away from the river. *CSH.*

Title trouble notwithstanding, no contradictory maps exist. Instead, Brighton's layout was corroborated a few years later in the Sacramento City assessor's map book, of all places. The usual record of properties within city limits are followed by dozens of blank pages, after which someone added a small collection of plats for properties mostly situated miles outside city jurisdiction. This collection included a three-page sketch of Brighton, less detailed but similar to the county record of 1851. The main difference was a reorientation of the racetrack and some missing riverfront blocks.[87]

Maps tucked away in the back of an official volume might raise eyebrows, but they certainly do not constitute an official record. These plats perhaps served some illegitimate purpose. Or they may be a good-faith response to the city's observation of poor county recordkeeping. The plats might even have been added to the book after the fact. Regardless, they seem to represent an organized and ongoing attempt at extralegal recordkeeping for unclear purposes; the same hand apparently reproduced much of this same extraneous collection for the 1855 map book. Brighton was omitted then, but blank pages within the collection seem hold its place. And one of these pages features the faint beginnings of a grid, in the same space filled by Brighton the previous year. The similarities between these collections strongly suggest that someone inside Sacramento City kept what appears to be ongoing records of property ownership well outside city limits.[88] Brighton's original form thus apparently enjoyed a degree of recognition at the city and county level. Someone responsible for tracking landownership saw reason to capture the shape of a community whose layout remained spatially consistent over several tumultuous years. Brighton's grid survived, on paper, for almost half a decade.

Furthermore, Brighton was not just an isolated grid. Both the 1854 and 1855 volumes depict an adjacent subdivision called Brighton Farms, stretching nearly three miles upstream and bisected by the ditch originally meant to provide water to Sutter's mill. These thirty-two farm plots started at forty acres, apparently the rural complement to an expected riverside city. The 1855 volume even records a solitary landowner whose name also appeared on Judah's plan: J.T. Day on Lot 8. Day's name is apparently written by a different hand than the map itself, hinting at a group within Sacramento City's government that tracked ownership of contested land well outside the city. A careful study of surviving city and county meeting minutes may yield enlightening clues about how these records relate to the unfolding "title trouble."

But where, exactly, did all this trouble unfold? Let us return to the original survey, with which geographic information system (GIS) software allows for a reasonably precise location of the town. A process called georeferencing is illustrated by the accompanying comparison with the Brighton area. The original map indicates the water's flow, confirming that Brighton stood on the river's left (south) bank, on a relatively straight stretch just upstream from a significant rightward bend. And when this map is oriented with the viewer facing due south, the arrangement fits its surroundings extraordinarily well, including the river curve and the track placement. Although the river's curve is inexact and its contours have certainly changed over nearly two centuries, it is nevertheless clear that Brighton lay just upstream of Sac State.

Brighton fits tidily into the Public Land Survey System (PLSS) survey framework. Brighton was "government land." Anyone who has flown in the United States knows this system by sight, if not name. Square-mile sections and 160-acre quarter-sections form a vast grid that became the standard for homesteading. The Brighton plat's details thus help confirm its probable location: It stretched from the river to 11th Street, with lateral streets lettered from A to T. The grid was composed of nearly two hundred square blocks.

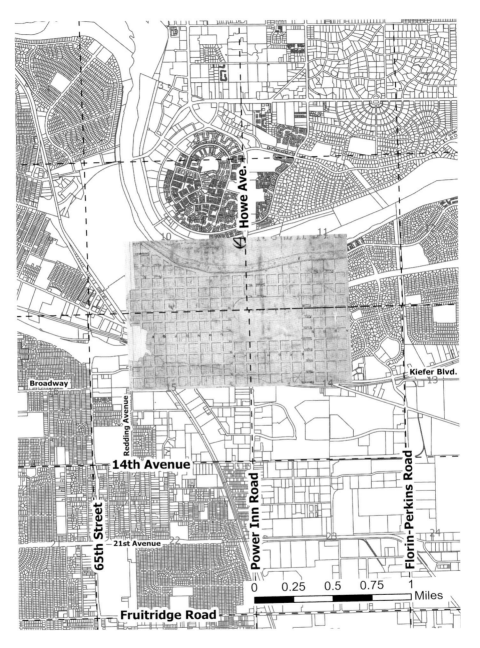

Proposed location of Brighton with current county parcel boundaries and the PLSS grid. Section-line roads are labeled, with half- and quarter-section labels smaller. *Andrew McLeod*.

Additional riverside blocks protrude from this rough rectangle, confirming Brighton's connection to the river bend. Crucially, T Street stretches precisely a mile north from a survey line, strongly suggesting its creators' intention to stake claims to government land defined by the PLSS. The mystery of how and why demands further research, but this grid seems to have been an intentional urban complement to the nation's dominant framework of rural land distribution, part of a thirty-six-square-mile township called T8N R5E.

Brighton was thus apparently platted out to serve as the front of the PLSS grid, right at the point that it collided with the crooked and chaotic subdivisions of Sutter's purported Mexican grant. Brighton had the PLSS in its DNA, with uniform blocks, 320 feet square, separated by 80-foot streets; the overall block interval was thus 400 feet in each direction, or just under one-thirteenth of a mile. The addition of an 80-foot perimeter road to a thirteen-block-square grid would extend exactly 5,280 feet—perfectly filling a one-square-mile section of an idealized township. Of course, conditions were hardly ideal in the Brighton vicinity.

But what might Brighton have become? A hint may be found in Kansas, a state where the PLSS grid dominates and where Sacramento's land struggles had an obscure but important influence. The PLSS grid is easily discernible in the modern city of Lawrence, much of which follows a rectangular subdivision of blocks measuring one-eighth by one-sixteenth of a mile. Although the calculations are different, this design is clearly akin to Brighton. But how might it have gotten from California to Kansas?

Sometime after the Settlers' military setback of August 1850 (which culminated in Brighton), association leader Dr. Charles Robinson departed Sacramento City, returned to Massachusetts and, after a quiet interlude, was recruited to spearhead the abolitionist colonization of Kansas; he led the establishment of Lawrence in 1854. Although no known evidence identifies Robinson's involvement in Brighton, he must have been attentive to a neighboring city where his comrades shot the sheriff. Robinson may not have directly transferred this model, but city grids composed of tidy PLSS fractions would be a likely hallmark of republican settlement design. This is how a city would look on "government land."

Early Brightonians probably assumed that their southern boundary road would connect to their town's hinterlands in the same way that Lawrence ultimately spread south and west from the Kansas River—homestead by homestead. But something halted Brighton's progress, and the probable town boundaries themselves show signs of disturbance.

In the proposed location, Brighton's southern boundary follows the same half-section line that extends eastward from Broadway and westward from Kiefer Boulevard. But both arteries are severed as they approach Brighton, leaving fragmentary parcel boundaries but no roads. Although gaps in rural road grids are common in the PLSS pattern, this concentration of gaps at exactly the place a road would be most useful is extraordinarily suspicious. Although Kiefer still meets Florin-Perkins Road south of the tracks, it stops before old Brighton. Broadway—which was still called Brighton Avenue in an 1888 ad for another failed town called Monte Vista—ends abruptly about a half-mile from city limits.[89] A few central blocks of 11th Street remain, redeployed as short and unattractive stretch of Folsom Boulevard that has encouraged generations of travelers to pass without stopping. On the west, Redding Avenue is apparently a disconnected remnant of T Street's southern end. The northern end of T, which once passed through the land now occupied by the university's student union, was entirely obliterated. Nothing exists of A Street on the east, despite Judah's 1854 map giving clear indications of major ongoing development in that corner of town nearest the ford.

This was not simply a matter of the Brighton property's subdivision being nullified, with some new owner taking possession and engaging with the surroundings with normal profit motives, under normal (albeit turbulent) circumstances. In that case, the border roads should have survived. Instead, the entirety of Brighton disappeared, connecting roads and all. And by all appearances, Brighton's disappearance was intentional.

THE TROUBLE WITH TITLE TROUBLE

The simplest explanation for Brighton's disappearance is that its promoters were selling property they didn't own. But if they didn't own it, who did? Sutter's mill attempt suggests that he fancied himself the landowner. There could have been rival claimants, but so far no specific rivals have emerged—only vague and unsupported assertions. Even if the supposed title trouble was that much of Brighton legitimately belonged to Sutter—which it did not—the southern and eastern portions of Brighton lay outside the land finally declared to be Sutter's by the U.S. Supreme Court in 1864. The justices drew an utterly absurd and arbitrary line around Section 10 of T8N R5E, legally carving off a corner of the city, roughly north of 4th and west of M. But the rest of Brighton should have survived if Sutter title was the problem—especially the upstream riverbank, which was home to the racetrack and most buildings mapped by Judah. The Supreme Court specifically declared that most of Brighton stood on government land. Yet the entire place disappeared as a whole, on both sides of this contrived line.

But what actually disappeared? Quite a lot. Physical developments in early Brighton are hard to square with the dismissive dominant narrative of some squatters on someone's land somewhere east of Sacramento City. For example, Charles Petit offered reminiscences to the *Sacramento Daily Union* four decades later. Identified as a major owner of Brighton on the Judah map, Petit recalled a small but significant community in November 1850, months after the Squatters' Riot:

> *At that time the town contained two large hotels, one of which was three stories in hight* [sic], *and it had over sixty rooms. There were also two large stores of miners' supplies, a blacksmith shop in an old adobe house, built either by General Sutter or some of his men, besides a number of private houses with families living in them. There were also town lots and corner lots for sale, and right back south of the town was the race track.*[90]

This all sounds solid enough, and many more details may be gleaned from accounts of Brighton's component structures.

The Pavilion Hotel was among the first buildings constructed on Brighton's main drag. It rose in 1849, perhaps even before Brighton was formally surveyed. This massive hotel was three stories in height, with a double balcony in front. The spacious barroom was very popular. The first floor contained public parlors and a reading room. On the second floor was the elegant dining and ballroom that had floor-to-ceiling windows that opened out onto the lower balcony. This floor also had private parlors for families and sleeping apartments. The third floor had more sleeping apartments.[91] After three years of operation, a fire burned the hotel, stables, outhouses and fences surrounding what the *Union* called "one of the handsomest and most commodious hotels in this section of the State."[92]

While it stood, the Pavilion's hosted many a racing fan, and development of the racetrack reinforced social and business connections despite rising intercity tension. The Brighton Jockey Club was organized July 1850, meeting in Sacramento City even as bloodshed loomed.[93] Construction of the track was completed early in the dark year of 1851, with the first races held over three days in May. During the grand launch, Birch & Company operated stages to Brighton from Sacramento City, departing from the

Orleans, the Sutter and the Crescent City Hotels every half hour.[94] Even then, after a year of turmoil and violence, at least some Sacramentans were still going all in with their Brighton wagers.

But within a year, the racecourse was listed for sale and apparently fell into neglect, according to the *Union*: "This favorite resort of the sporting circles, has recently been ploughed, harrowed and sowed with barley, and already the verdant spears are peeping from the ground, leaving no traces of the track over which the fleet coursers so lately sped."[95] But not so fast! Only weeks later, the track hosted a $2,000 purse event that surely damaged this tender crop.[96] And the oval that appears on two different 1854 maps shows that race days were far from over.

And of course there was Allen's inn, Brighton's most notorious location and the site of the sheriff's death. Initial ambush reporting by the *Transcript* indicated that it was located "two or three houses past the Pavilion."[97] Owner James Allen was wounded and fled across the river. But he returned after an apparent sojourn in the mines, showing that both he and the Settlers were not done in Brighton. Years later, Petit recalled a house along the river and an eroding cluster of graves that held "the remains of the Allen party."[98] The squatters stuck around even after death, and Brighton would not go down easily.

REBEL-HELD TERRITORY

For such a lively place, scholarship on Brighton is extraordinarily sparse. In 2016, Thomas J. Savage glanced at Brighton, offering a few details to set the scene for a study of a Mormon couple living there. Despite Brighton serving merely as a backdrop to the topic at hand, this remains one of the most attentive secondary sources known. Savage describes the origins of the place as a small Mormon settlement and notes that the Brighton Eating House began advertising in October 1849, "at the crossing of the American Fork, 4 miles from Sacramento City."[99] Savage also claims that Gelston bought the land directly from Sutter in January 1850, but unfortunately his cited source here does not specifically mention this event that would profoundly affect ownership questions. Savage also doubts that Brighton was a viable port, dismissing Gelston's big spring shipment as a "publicity stunt."[100]

Paula Peper gave the most recent focused attention in her 2009 book *Sacramento's Brighton Township: Stories of the Land*, which was produced to promote the redevelopment of the area. Peper's work is highly problematic but provides a useful sample of the dominant narrative's rampant inaccuracies. For example, Peper incorrectly asserts that Sutter's grant stretched all the way to Bradshaw Road.[101] This would be miles beyond even the Supreme Court's absurdly generous 1864 ruling. Peper also repeats Thompson & West's false assertion that Brighton was "[a]bandoned by the end of 1852 due to land trouble including what was termed 'defective titles.'"[102]

Subsequent events clearly reveal this recycled claim of abandonment to be premature. In reality, Brightonians stood and fought using a variety of tactics, including legal action, mutual aid and at least the threat of violence. In 1853, settlers in Brighton formed the Brighton Township Association. On September 24, they gathered at A.D. Patterson's (near the old mill intake at modern Bradshaw Road) to form "an association for our mutual protection against the avaricious speculators of California, but more particularly against those of Sacramento county."[103]

Tensions escalated thenceforth. In December 1854, Allen returned. This notorious squatter ally sought to reclaim his 160 acres from Colonel Alpheus Kipp, who was predictably unwilling to yield possession. Allen then returned with associates and lumber to build a house. The *Union* fretted: "The dispute will doubtless end in a law suit."[104] Appeals to law were perhaps overly optimistic; Allen was, after all, squatting the same land on which the sheriff was once killed by insurgents whom Allen was harboring. And the authorities in Sacramento City were apparently powerless to stop him or the provocation that followed: In May 1855, settlers strung up six effigies across the plank road, including U.S. Supreme Court Chief Justice Roger Taney, along with an ex-governor, a senator and a few federal land commissioners. This "deeply mortifying news" served as a blunt reminder of Sacramento City's limited power in this restive suburb.[105]

Brighton's settlers also acted less symbolically. In February 1857, a group including Allen sought to collectively purchase the land they were occupying. They offered ten dollars per acre to anyone who could present a clear and undisputed title. "We make this proposition because we consider it a liberal one, under the circumstances, as the land has been rendered valuable by our labor, and because we wish to avoid law suits," they announced. As to who really owned the land, they said they would let the adverse claimants work it out among themselves.[106]

Resolution remained elusive. In the summer of 1857, tension between the Brighton settlers and Sacramento City officials rose again when Samuel Norris obtained a District Court order that forbade settlers from harvesting on land that he claimed to be his own. The *Sacramento Bee* ran an editorial the next day warning

> *that a serious difficulty may occur before long between a portion of the Settlers of this county on the one side, and the constituted authorities on the other...the Settlers say, and say it boldly, that they will not suffer their own or their neighbors' property to be thus taken from them—that their crops are all they have, and that, if needs be, they may as well die defending them as die because they did not defend them.*[107]

Brighton was thus clearly not abandoned. And the fight was more than just a bunch of scrappy farmers grubbing for land. In 1862, a new front opened in the struggle for control of the region's wealth extraction apparatus, with Brighton right in the middle of it. After years of conflict, Sacramento City demanded that the Sacramento Valley Railroad remove its tracks west of 6th Street, making California's first rail system nearly useless. The company then attempted to bypass Sacramento City entirely, with a branch line from Brighton to a new railhead at Freeport.[108] When completed in 1863, the ten-mile line ended at a major new wharf facility for passengers and freight.[109] But the Central Pacific purchased the system in 1866 and dismantled the entire investment. Freeport, like Brighton, returned to agriculture.[110] A major regional asset was thereby destroyed, despite its vast potential value of spreading commerce beyond a single flood-prone port. The West's first railroad was neutralized and, later, reduced to a spur of the transcontinental line. If Sacramento City couldn't have the benefit of rail to the Mother Lode, no one could.

Nowadays, Sacramentans shrug and recall vaguely that Brighton had some title trouble. The process by which such proposed trouble was resolved is murky at best. Such an assertion requires much more support than previously offered. Further research is needed, but the preceding sample of news stories shows that Brighton was not abandoned. It remained contested land for most of a decade, with multiple parties seeking control of valuable real estate. It was apparently a durable center of resistance to Sacramento City. And then it disappeared.

Similar events just downstream, on a different piece of land with a different constellation of adverse claimants, raise further questions. The stories of Norristown and Hoboken reveal a larger and more complicated dynamic to the east of Sacramento City, in which the control of levees and bridges became a weapon of intercity conflict.

CHAPTER 4
NORRISTOWN AND HOBOKEN

By Andrew McLeod

In 1853, flooding again drove Sacramento City's population to high ground. Many people landed about five miles east, along with a large portion of the city's businesses. The resulting community was known as Hoboken, which is generally (if faintly) recalled as an ephemeral tent encampment that dried up as quickly as the waters fell. But this same riverbank was already home to another town, founded in 1850 just downstream from Brighton and touted as nearly immune to flooding. Norristown's remnants apparently provided the core of permanent buildings depicted by the *Sacramento Union* as a "View of Hoboken," which suggests continuous occupation of a winning location that enjoyed excellent access by land and water, as well as low flood hazard.

This durable double settlement has been hiding in plain sight all along, tucked behind the levee that rings East Sacramento. Although nearly invisible to history, Norristown and Hoboken appear in numerous primary sources, beginning with Samuel Norris's 1849 land purchase from Johann Sutter and continuing to the present. They appear in newspapers, maps and—surprisingly—aerial photographs. Even currently valid parcel boundaries pinpoint Norristown's footprint. The region's historic narrative fails to explain this faint but persistent presence.

Norristown stood just upstream from a river crossing that led to one of the region's first settler farms. This was a central location on the American River's natural levee, facing deep and relatively quiet water. As Sacramentans waited here for the 1853 flood to recede, they had plenty of time to ponder the location's superiority to those chaotic bottomlands a few miles down the road. Norristown must have appeared among the region's safest land investments and safest homes.

So why did everyone apparently leave after the early 1850s? Nobody knows. Norristown has apparently never been seriously studied.[111] The only findable academic mention is a mere flicker in a 1946 biographical article about its founder, "Samuel Norris: Litigious Pioneer." Allen L. Chickering's article recalls that Norris laid out a town with "regular" steamboat service and leaves it at that.[112] As for Norristown's successor, the most significant attention came in 1967 when Walter Frame wrote "Fires, Floods and Hoboken," a *Golden Notes* pamphlet for the Sacramento County Historical Society. His analysis will be discussed shortly. Most recently, *A History of the Lower American River* (1977, revised in 1991) makes passing reference to Norristown in the context of flooding: Samuel Norris saw opportunity in Sacramento City's vulnerability, but his namesake is erroneously dismissed as "a paper city only."[113] Nothing seems to have been published for the last half century.

This sparse historiography spans only three decades out of the nearly twenty that have passed. The only serious attention to Hoboken (and Norristown, barely) came during the 1970s. Historians have thus failed to reckon with a community that apparently lasted for several of Sacramento's most formative years. Three known sources apparently represent the only mentions of early settlement of the area now mostly occupied by the Sacramento State University, despite a major road that once passed just outside the windows of its History Department.

It is high time for another look at a story mixing the western and mystery genres. This site was a good alternative to the swampy and contested wetlands of Sacramento City—a speculative scheme that ultimately became California's capital. Yet Norristown and Hoboken were wiped off the map, in a subplot of the gold rush land saga that has evaded the faintest flicker of collective memory.

THE DARK SIDE OF THE LEVEE

A flood-control structure ironically destroyed one of the region's best flood refuges. The Sacramento City community's 1853 relocation to Hoboken shows that this riverbank was less prone to inundation than its downstream neighbor—and known to be so! Norristown perched on the American River's natural levee, atop a broad hill that crested above thirty-five feet in elevation. This hill was ten feet higher than the lofty perch of Sutter's Fort and as much as twenty feet above Sacramento City. Norristown's natural advantage was therefore crystal clear. Its topography should have ensured some degree of persistent settlement regardless of any known social, political or economic dynamics.

This riverbank wasn't perfect, of course. Whenever the American River overflowed, water had to pass through and around Norristown before coursing into the Sacramento City flood basin. This water moved through a pair of sloughs named Sutter and Burns, which would have been wet and flood-prone.[114] In addition to whatever water jumped the river's southern bank, any rain falling on a roughly mile-wide strip would drain through Norristown. The south and west sides of town were therefore poor places to live despite the site's general advantages.

These troublesome sloughs became a much bigger problem in the 1860s, when they were blocked by the construction of a storage spur for the transcontinental railroad. The new tracks were perched atop a massive levee, connected to the Southern Pacific's B Street line between the railroad shops and the crossing near modern Cal Expo. A parallel siding would be more

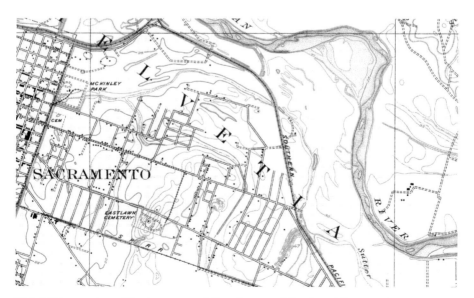

This 1911 map shows Norristown on a hilltop but cut off by the rail levee and separated from new growth in East Sacramento. *USGS.*

typical, and this perpendicular, elevated alignment belies another purpose: protecting Sacramento City. As shown by the elevation map in chapter 1, the spur stretched southeasterly toward high ground, putting both Norristown and Brighton on the wrong side of the levee. Even routine flow of Sutter and Burns Sloughs was now blocked, redirecting water downstream. Flooding in Norristown must have worsened dramatically, presenting any holdout residents with a hazardous and isolated future.

A levee closer to the river would have been on higher ground. It would have needed less material to reach a comparable elevation and protected more land, including a town founded by one of interior California's first pioneers. But after levee construction, flooding was stuck in Norristown instead of following the ancient sloughs to the basin in which Sacramento City lay. Water would now pool at the levee and then flow parallel to the river's main channel until the large westward bend now called Paradise Beach. This levee thereby created a major hazard for anyone still living at the very spot at which Sacramentans originally escaped that same hazard. What was previously the highest and safest land around was now threatened by even moderate winter runoff, due to a levee that was more costly and less effective than if it had been built closer to the river. Land in Norristown's western slough corridor would certainly have been cheaper to acquire, but this placement suggests that Sacramento City weaponized flood control to eliminate a competitor that had already shown itself to be a much better location for riding out the valley's volatile winter floods.

Robert Kelley's *Battling the Inland Sea* provides an excellent study of how levee construction often harmed neighbors upstream and across-stream. Such conflicts involved force at least once, as discussed in a chapter colorfully titled "The Parks Dam War."[115] But did Norristown actually have permanent residents for an analogous war, or was it merely a long-gone paper town? The bulk of evidence points toward a town that functioned for at least a few years as an orderly settlement on a specific subdivided piece of land.

MAPPING A PHANTOM

Norristown is occasionally caught lurking on the fringes of Sacramento cartography. Its most prominent appearance came in 1913, two years after a large annexation extended Sacramento city limits to the railroad levee whose spikes perhaps doubled as the nails in Norristown's coffin.[116] The *Map of Sacramento City*, published by Phinney, Cate & Marshall, depicts an expanding city in great detail while also reminding viewers what came before by superimposing disappeared settlements.[117] Norristown appears on mostly empty land northeast of the railroad tracks, split into two riverside tracts totaling almost half a square mile.

Norristown's lingering boundaries clash with then-current features. This shows some sort of rupture in ordinary development patterns in which major roads often form along boundaries of large properties, which are later subdivided. Instead, "N.W. Corner of Norristown" juts awkwardly into the Wright Tract. And "S.W. Cor. of Norristown" intrudes on the properties of East Sacramento's old Italian farm district. Both corners cross the railroad and are isolated from the rest of the town's original rectangular tract.

Lines on a map do not always mark real features on the ground, especially in Gold Rush Sacramento. The 1913 depiction also suggests that whatever once existed in Norristown was obliterated by that date; even unusually inquisitive cartographers failed to locate any plats confirming streets and parcels. So to discern what stood in Norristown before it became farmland—still worth mapping decades later—we must look both backward and forward in time.

Four types of early historic evidence confirm Norristown as a real and somewhat durable settlement. First, newspapers captured signs of civic life and raised no known questions about the underlying title—despite that being a common theme of the period's real estate news and an accepted cause of neighboring Brighton's demise.[118] Second, an extraneous Pony Express stop suggests a lasting population center throughout the 1850s. Third, Norristown appears explicitly on at least one map drawn nearly a decade after its founding, confirming stable boundaries. Finally, real estate deeds use Norristown as a point of reference, suggesting that its location remained a relatively uncontested matter of fact in subsequent decades.

Three types of post-1913 evidence confirm Norristown's unlikely persistence. First, aerial photos clearly show remnants of city limits that were still visible at flight altitude a century later. Second, a Depression-era survey pinpoints a corner being ingested by the City of Sacramento. Finally, current parcel boundaries explicitly refer to Norristown.

Phinney, Cate & Marshall had good reason to believe that there was something worth remembering.

Norristown's first surviving mention appeared in March 1850, when an advertisement in the *Placer Times* boasted of a "splendid town site…much higher than the late flood which inundated Sacramento City." Readers were reminded that the road to the mining district passed through, while river

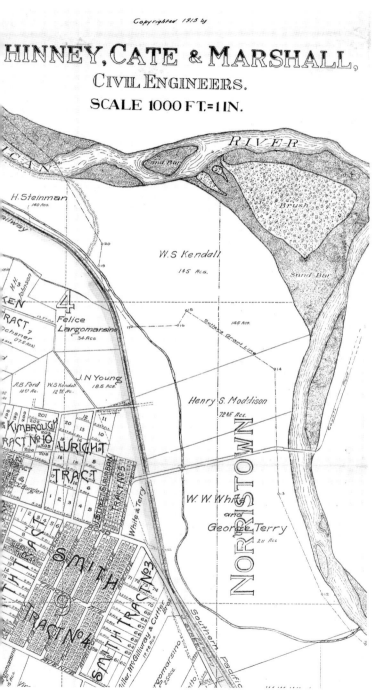

Phinney, Cate & Marshall's 1913 *Map of Sacramento City* precisely locates the edges and corners of Norristown, superimposed against properties recently annexed by Sacramento. *CSH.*

access was available "the greater portion of the year." A leading Sacramento City land merchant named Henry Schoolcraft offered a map for inspection by interested parties.[119] But was Norristown merely platted out on speculation, with no expectation that it would survive longer than needed to turn a profit in the crazed gold rush real estate market? That may be. Newspapers of the day brimmed with glowing descriptions of dismal bottomlands for sale.

But Norristown was apparently a budding center of business and politics. In late April, the steamboat *Etna* was making regular arrivals from Sacramento City.[120] Such commercial transit service might not have been viable year-round, but people were certainly coming by water that spring. Norristown was also a rising civic center, serving as one of eight precincts for the first county election that same month.[121] And when six county districts were established in May, one was "Norristown and the settlements adjacent thereto."[122] Norristown was clearly a significant secondary hub for the emerging population center at Sacramento City.

Norristown also engaged in national politics. On the Fourth of July, "Captain Samuel Norris" fired the cannon, joining Sacramento City, Sutterville, Sutter's Fort and Brighton in an explosive morning observance.[123] Settlers in a wild land still awaiting statehood must have felt some comfort in hearing these coordinated blasts booming out over the swamplands, tying together far-flung infant communities into a single American celebration.

Then there was silence. Norristown suddenly vanished from the surviving collection of newspapers, right when it should have been most newsworthy. No surviving report recalls title disputes, business failures or even boats running aground as the river dropped that summer. Meanwhile, tensions rose as Sacramento careened toward August's settler uprising, which must have given many people second thoughts about the increasingly dominant bottomland neighbors, still recovering from the winter's flooding. Notably, the *Placer Times* disappears from preserved collections at approximately the same time (June 7), despite its continued operation for another year. Missing issues may contain clues to this former advertiser's sudden demise.

Yet somehow a remnant held on. The 1860 location of the "Five Mile Station" suggests concentrated settlement lasting at least a decade. California Registered Historical Landmark No. 697 stands at the western end of the Guy West bicycle bridge—near where the J Street Road once met the river. Although Pony Express stations were typically spaced at fifteen-mile intervals, this was an additional station close to Sacramento City.[124] A horse would barely break a sweat after this short leg on relatively flat terrain. So why change mounts here? The best explanation is that this was a population center at which eastbound mail was gathered and waiting, or quickly dropped before the final westward gallop to Sacramento City.

Meanwhile, despite studious editorial avoidance of Norristown reporting, the name continued to appear in newsprint. Real estate notices confirm that this tract remained a significant landmark from which other property boundaries were derived. One strange but prominent example was a sheriff's sale notice in November 1855. The southeast corner of Norristown was also the easternmost reference point of the "Larco Line," which marked out a vast triangular tract that stretched to the Sacramento River near Freeport.[125] Larco's name is generally unfamiliar to Sacramento historians, despite his apparently successful challenge to Sutter's unrestrained acquisitiveness. The basis for Larco's claim remains unknown, but his line appears with on a bizarre, ragged specimen held by the California State Library. *Map of the Partition Between Sanders & Muldrow, in October 1858 and May 1860* seems to record agreements made by two audacious investors in the land market, divvying up their targets on a broad wedge of land between the rivers. Although unorthodox in origin and incoherent in places, this map clearly

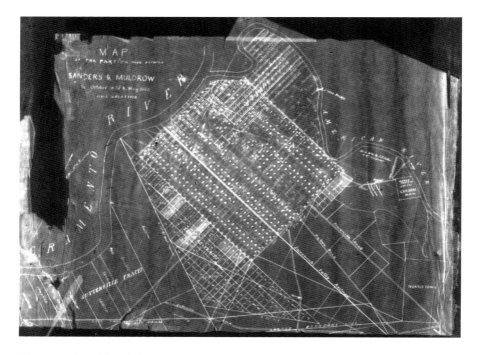

The mysterious *Map of the Partition Between Sanders & Muldrow* is held by the State Library despite unclear origins and very poor condition. *CSL.*

shows a Norristown similar to that recalled in 1913. Hoboken is also labeled, faintly, just upstream.[126]

We might dismiss these marks as the mad scribbles of rogue speculators. Or we might seek other sources for confirmation or contradiction. The county assessor's annual map books should detail how land changed hands from year to year. These books once provided a visual account of how property holdings evolved and would have depicted detailed subdivision and sales within the Norristown tract. Unfortunately, no volumes remain from the county's first twenty years. By the first surviving record in 1870, Norristown was intact and entirely owned by the Sacramento Valley Beet Sugar Company, on both sides of the tracks (suggesting ownership prior to railroad construction).[127] Sowing and harvesting a root crop would quickly and handily obscure any archaeological features.

Whatever might have been plowed under afterward, Norristown was built on a legal foundation that originated with Sutter himself—for better or worse. This was among the county's oldest surveyed properties, with hints of American settlement well before the gold. This trail back to Norristown's origins begins in 1852, when Gregory Phelan purchased most of modern East Sacramento from Eugene Gillespie (along with Elmhurst and everything from the old fairgrounds to Alhambra Boulevard). The survey "commenc[ed] at the southeast corner of a tract of land sold by John A. Sutter to Samuel Norris…commonly known as Norristown." This description takes pains to affirm legitimacy of its eastern boundary by citing the 1849 Sutter deed.[128]

Schoolcraft signed that prior deed as Sutter's attorney, perhaps already tallying up his future profits from a choice subdivision. The price was $2,000—a nice pile in those days. It is unclear what Sutter originally paid for this strategic property, but most likely the price was not a serious valuation for this nearly flood-proof crossroads. The Nisenan surely took whatever they were offered, if anything was offered at all. Ironically, the 1849 deed notes a carve-out around the "Kanaka Houses," indicating a community of Hawaiians lived here. The Nisenan were offered no such reserve.

The Norristown tract straddled the natural levee route following the American River's southern bank—and not just anywhere along that thoroughfare. Sutter's deed confirms that this was an important crossroads property, beginning at "the present old ford or ferry landing, formerly known as Sinclair's ferry." Norristown's downstream border therefore followed an established passage from the north side of the river. Its name suggests establishment around 1842, when historian Cheryl Anne Stapp recalls John and Mary Sinclair "took possession" of the Del Paso Grant, which they

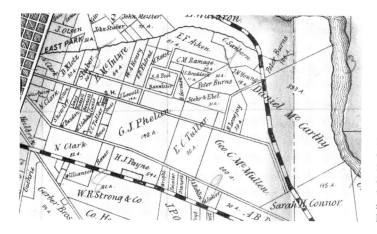

This 1885 county map shows a remnant of the road to Sinclair's crossing, branching north from J Street. Both thoroughfares were severed by the levee. *LOC.*

were already farming just north of the floodplain now known as Campus Commons.[129] Norris himself makes only minor appearances in Stapp's *Before the Gold Rush*, and she never mentions his town across the river. However, she acknowledges that Norris owned the rancho in 1849, a year before he launched Norristown.[130] Stapp also reproduces her personal copy of an 1844 diseño showing three buildings just east of the river's most prominent bend—probably the Sinclair farm later occupied by Norris.[131]

This "old ford" thus connected the twin centers of European settlement in the area—Sutter and Sinclair. It was probably a much older thoroughfare for humans and animals alike, connecting high ground relatively close to both sides of the river. Although the ancient path surely meandered and branched, Norristown's straight right-of-way funneled traffic more than a kilometer along its northern edge, up "to a post on the prairie," an arc of high land running nearly a mile west and a mile south.[132] The initial survey of Norristown therefore marked a major regional intersection that would have been an excellent bypass of Sacramento City.

Furthermore, part of this boundary persisted long after Norristown's disappearance. An official 1885 county map shows a branch jogging northward from the J Street Road—a few blocks up modern 53rd and then east on F to dead-end at the tracks. This feature's symbology resembles that of J Street itself, suggesting a major route without a destination. Just upstream on the same map, J Street has its own troubles: Sacramento City's original straight shot to the mines, the original Pony Express route, was now forced southward along the tracks, cutting through old Norristown's landward remnant to a humiliating dead end at Sarah H. Connor's property line. This is a strange state of affairs for what was once a pair of fundamental roadways.

Modern County Records

People make maps for a reason, and they must choose what to include or exclude. Paying attention to what is mapped and what is not mapped can provide candid glimpses into how departed generations saw the world around them. Even without a mapmaker's written thoughts, we may still discern cartographic motives. An unusually clear example came a half-century after the county mapped Norris's blocked crossing.

In 1933, Sacramento's city surveyor, F.J. Klaus, surveyed a portion of the northern boundary of Norristown, along with its northwestern corner. He pinpointed the latter on the southern edge of F Street, 88.07 feet eastward from 54th Street's midline. Other similarly precise measurements detail Norristown's relationship to the overlaid subdivision.[133] And Klaus did not incidentally capture an obscure historic feature; this official survey was titled *Plat of Survey Showing Location of North-West Corner of "Norristown"* after all. Klaus meant to locate a foundational point of reference.

Why did Klaus survey Norristown in 1933? He presumably had a very specific reason for devoting public resources to precisely locating this shard

In 1933. F.J. Klaus surveyed the corner of Norristown, pinpointing the intersection of F Street with the town's northern line and river crossing access. *CSH.*

of a dead city, two decades after it became embedded in his own. Aerial imagery from 1937 reveals that this parcel approached an irregular crossing to a well-used road that is now River Park's Messina Way. Perhaps there was some question about how this now-severed road crossed over the levee before jogging back north to rejoin the old Norristown border road on its

Norristown remnants are still visible in 1937, with an informal rail crossing at its northern edge and a small triangular parcel at its southwest corner. *UCSB.*

way to the old ford. This last wedge of old Norristown provided access over the rails and stood in the way of a thoroughfare to be built a dozen years hence. Clearly something was amiss as the last life was squeezed out of this ancient river access. By midcentury, construction of Elvas Avenue finally finished it off.

Nowadays, nothing remains of Norristown's western edge, which faces East Sacramento along an expressway that is itself tangled and confusing where it trips over intersecting roads that eventually reconnected Sacramento to lands across the river. Norristown's upstream, southern boundary has now been largely erased by the development of the university, leaving only faint marks on the levees flanking campus.[134] This old boundary road remained until at least 1937. Remnant property lines suggest that Norristown's easternmost corner was an important landmark on the banks of the American River. Even today, the County Assessor's website shows fragments of several property lines, and at least one road headed toward the spot where Norristown met Brighton.[135]

Only one tangible patch of southern Norristown has survived. A small bungalow now occupies a triangular lot at 63rd and Elvas. This half-acre wedge, just southwest of the tracks, is bounded on the south by a line dating to the gold rush—confirmed by the County Assessor's description of two nearby industrial parcels in relation to a point "276.50 ft from SW cor Norristown."[136] Modern legal descriptions thus pinpoint, within inches, the location of Norristown's original boundaries. The extremities of this durable tract of land, first described in 1849, are still intact. The title underlying Norristown survived decades of turmoil in the region and remains a legal feature 175 years after its creation. Norristown was therefore a coherent and specific property, which mostly survived for a century before its second subdivision. This raises the question of what happened during Norristown's first subdivision: Why did a pioneer town become farmland for nearly a century before it was donated for a college campus?

High and Dry

Given the high inherent value of the land and at least two major settlement attempts, some remains of economic development should exist. At the very least, the waterfront should recall some kind of riparian industry. Yet there are no pilings, no foundations, no sign that anyone ever made a sustained attempt to develop this prime location during the first century of American settlement. Although the shallow river channel downstream would have blocked larger watercraft in the summer and fall, Norristown faced a stretch of river resembling a narrow lake. Water was deep even in the summer, with a relatively gentle current during the floods that repeatedly devastated downstream neighbors.[137] Someone could have made extraordinary profits carving up this riverbank astride what was briefly one of the world's most dynamic trade routes.

The lack of any historic infrastructure here is simply bizarre. And only one historian has ever inquired about this. But even he left out most of the picture. In "Fire, Floods & Hoboken," Walter Frame claimed that "Norristown failed to prosper, and prior to 1852 the only building on the property was a wayside inn known as the Four Mile House," just west on J Street.[138] This error was corrected right alongside Frame's writing by an accompanying image titled "View of Hoboken, on the American River." This depiction contradicts his assertion that only one nearby building survived, standing just outside of Norristown limits. Smoke rises from chimneys on a pair of two-story wood-frame buildings, right in the center of town. What's more, the strip of permanent structures seems to continue along the same line beyond these buildings, stretching out of sight behind the tents at right.[139] The triangular shape of the image's crowded streetscape is consistent with two converging grids arrayed along a convex river bend, with the older grid continuing beyond the vertex where two competing city limits apparently crossed (assuming the prior chapter's proposed Brighton placement). This image therefore seems to capture the view of the present college campus looking northeast from the fitness center toward the student union.

Hoboken is generally understood to have lasted only for weeks during early 1853, so at least two blocks of dense urban streetscape demands some explanation. These structures were certainly not constructed during a flood and appear to follow a single straight roadway. They most likely survived from the Norristown period. This suggests ongoing economic and social activity, reframing Hoboken's demise as much more than everyone simply breaking camp after a few soggy weeks. This was the death of an orderly settlement that had lasted for years.

Or maybe it was murder. Indeed, Frame asks whether this was a "deliberate act of urbicide."[140] He blames Hoboken's demise on flood damage at Lisle's Bridge downstream at Sacramento City—the drawbridge was nailed shut, effectively ending commercial river traffic. This would have been a severe blow to any towns upstream, but Frame missed an important part of the story. Although flood damage may well have impeded travel along the

The *Sacramento Union*'s 1853 depiction of Hoboken captures a string of wood-frame buildings that apparently stood along Norristown's upstream boundary. *UCB.*

American River, news reports indicate a more menacing sort of trouble. On January 5, 1853, the county supervisors heard a delegate's alarming report that the main bridge "was guarded by an armed force, who refused to raise the draw, or allow me to raise it….Consequently it is at present a great obstruction to business."[141] The board promptly passed a resolution for the sheriff to deliver, demanding that the draw be opened at once. And that was apparently the end of that. The *Union* never reported whether the armed force was ever dislodged from its barricade.

Norristown's land access was likewise disrupted. The J Street Road was severed with little or no public discussion, cutting the main route into Norristown and Brighton, thence upstream to Coloma. This would be akin to the quiet removal of modern U.S. Highway 50. The old thoroughfare was thenceforth diverted southward along the rails, and for most of a century, all traffic headed east was forced through a single crossing at Folsom Boulevard, which remains the only non-freeway thoroughfare on the river's south side (and an extraordinarily inhospitable streetscape).

Whoever was responsible, Thompson & West's 1880 drawing of Daniel McCarty's ranch provides a clear image of the resulting scene. Not only does J Street make a clearly unnatural turn south, but a three-story building stands right in its former path, ensuring that the crossing would remain closed. No

Thompson and West's 1880 depiction of Daniel McCarty's ranch shows the old J Street Road forced to turn abruptly southward at the railroad levee. *SPL.*

hint of human construction appears beyond the tracks. The river is visible, but nothing crosses the conspicuously featureless private pastureland toward the old ford. McCarty was presumably content with this depiction—and disruption—to the land he acquired in 1878.

But then McCarty went rogue, with the first sign of trouble emerging at a 1901 meeting of Sacramento's city trustees. A levee inspection had discovered a fence erected across the tracks.[142] Such a discovery raises two important questions: First, why was the fence not first detected by an engineer picking barbed wire out of their cow-catcher? The rails must have been lightly used at best. Second, why was the discovery not the end of the story? Under normal circumstances, the Southern Pacific would have cleared the obstruction in less time than it took to set type. Surely "the Octopus" had some wire cutters lying around in its vast shops complex downtown. Instead, the matter drew more than a year of journalistic attention. McCarty's suit against the Southern Pacific Company et al. would ensnare the city of Sacramento and neighboring landowners and complicate efforts to move rail traffic off the old R Street line. By 1902, the *Bee* was reporting, "The claim of the city to the possession of this strip for levee purposes was seriously contested by the plaintiff," suggesting significant legal doubts regarding the right of way.[143]

Although this major legal episode faded from Sacramento's collective memory, some still remembered Norristown and Hoboken in the 1880s. The *Union* printed two such reminiscences of 1853, affirming that the two names were closely linked. First, I.N. Hoag recalled, "Wholesale business in Sacramento was almost entirely transferred to points on the American river...and the ferryboat Beta was pretty busy during January and February in freighting goods from Sacramento to Hoboken and Norristown."[144] And E.S. Hall remembered a trip toward Sacramento to get supplies: "I did not reach your city because I found your merchants, with their goods, on the south bank of the American River, in tents at Norristown."[145]

Many people lived in Norristown and Hoboken for years. They ate, slept, fought and loved here. They remembered the place, but those memories never made it into history in any significant way. Something blocked them out.

The strange tale of Norristown and Hoboken is difficult to square with establishment history. But traces remain scattered through the primary sources despite obvious gaps in the story. This was simply an excellent place for a city, at least relative to its hazardous surroundings. The question of who killed these towns—and how they did it—is a matter for further research. Despite its obvious natural advantages, an attractive site was depopulated and kept empty for a century, until most was donated to the state for a university campus and part was converted to postwar suburban housing. One of Sacramento's major early suburbs disappeared into the shadow of a levee, never to emerge.

CHAPTER 5

WHERE THE UPLAND MINERS LIVED

By Eric Webb

MINING TOWNS AS COMPANY TOWNS

Even as the erstwhile California Gold Rush towns of Negro Hill and Mormon Island rest submerged at the bottom of Folsom Lake, an apt comparison can be found between them and Minnesota's "twin cities" of Minneapolis and St. Paul. Entwined by geography, with only the south fork of the American River separating the two California mining towns, each couplet features one town that has been celebrated as much as the other ignored or maligned.

Although the seat of state government, St. Paul has long languished in the shadow of its neighbor. In recent decades, however, Minnesota's capital city has been heralded for its diversity and affordability. It has also gained a measure of prestige. Minneapolis may have the Guthrie Theater, but St. Paul is the stomping ground for *A Prairie Home Companion*. Conversely, Negro Hill has a higher hill to climb with California's collective memory, especially in relation to its bigger sibling, Mormon Island. Yet just as with St. Paul, glimmers of light have appeared in recent years.

The historical record favors Mormon Island. Virtually every photograph is taken from its perspective, and other than accounts of racial violence, very few journalists paid attention to the community of Negro Hill. Though fragmented, historical treatments of Mormon Island abound, whereas Negro Hill largely has been ignored, only meriting a scant half-page mention in an 1883 history of El Dorado County. Even as the nearby Coloma Road enjoyed

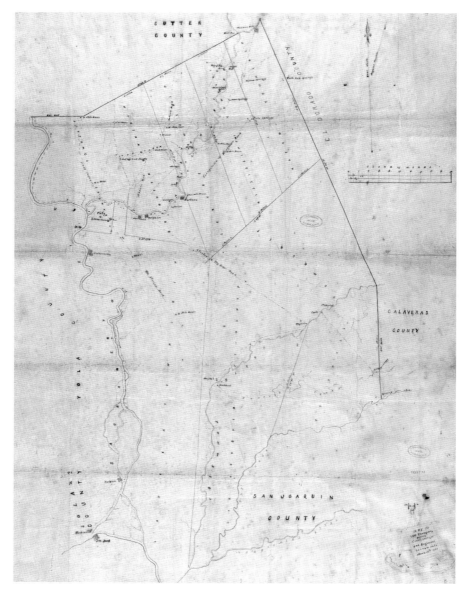

An 1851 map of Mormon Island, Negro Hill and the surrounding region. *CSL.*

demarcation on local maps, Negro Hill Road, also known as the El Dorado Turnpike during its heyday in the mid-1850s, did not. Yet with a quick peek underneath the surface, the historian discovers numerous references to this busy thoroughfare, including in the advertisements of stage lines.

Contemporary accounts, most especially the epistles of Newton Miller, shed light on the vibrant, multiracial community of Negro Hill in the 1850s. Black entrepreneurs prevailed along with a small yet thriving Chinatown, and by mid-decade, the twin cities of Mormon Island and Negro Hill contained a combined population of nearly four thousand.[146] Meanwhile, nearby Prairie City caught up with its neighbors as it ballooned to two thousand residents in 1853. By the 1856 election, Prairie City had the largest voting precinct in the county outside of Sacramento City.[147]

The three towns were not only among the largest of the gold fields, they were also the most historically significant. Mormon Island was the birthplace of the Natoma Mining and Water Company (NMWC), which molded the region into a center for hydrologic engineering, initially for mining interests, subsequently for agriculture. Founded in 1851 by Amos Catlin, a wealthy attorney from upstate New York, the company gobbled up its competitors and amassed extensive real estate holdings as it evolved into a Gilded Age juggernaut.

Water rights were at least as valuable as real estate. Citing an unpublished history of the NMWC from the 1980s, recent historians have summed up its acquisitions of the nineteenth century, often referred to as the "Natoma purchase," thusly:[148]

> To understand placer mining in the Folsom region one must understand the Natoma Water and Mining Company, one of the earliest corporations in California and one of the longest lasting. The NMWC was organized by A.P. Catlin during the early period of capitalist development and corporate organization in California's boom and bust mining economy. It was one of the earliest to incorporate explicitly for the purpose of transporting and selling water, and, during its first years of existence, it acquired title to extensive water rights and thousands of acres of land along the American River.[149]

The NMWC was one of the first companies in California to apply advanced engineering principles as it constructed what became known colloquially as the Natoma Ditch, a spider web of canals, tunnels and wooden flumes, some spanning more than one hundred feet, the "ditch" crisscrossed more than one hundred miles along the American River and beyond. The main canal, which hugged the south fork of the American River, was eight feet wide at the top, five feet wide at the base and three feet deep. It stretched for sixteen miles, with fifty miles of branches.[150]

Water was the lifeblood of mining, and it quickly became a valuable commodity: "By the end of the 1850s, over 750 water companies in California had built almost 6,000 miles of ditches, canals and flumes at a cost of over $13 million."[151] At the conclusion of 1853, the NMWC had spent a staggering amount of money on the Natoma Ditch, more than $1.5 million for diversion projects on the American River alone.[152] This engineering project was the most ambitious of the early California Gold Rush and offered a blueprint for the Central Valley Project of the twentieth century.

The importance of the NMWC cannot be overstated, with its handprints impressed on every regional water project of the late nineteenth and twentieth centuries as it provided Folsom with drinking water through the 1940s. Numerous Sacramento area water districts can trace their history to the Natoma Company, which operated for 133 years until it closed shop in 1984. Even after the town of Prairie City was degazetted in 1883, the NMWC supplied water to the general area, the last active gold field in the Sacramento region, employing myriad intensive mining techniques such as bucket line and dragline dredging.[153] Simultaneously, the NMWC oversaw numerous agricultural projects, including a two-thousand-acre vineyard, "at one point in the 1880s the largest in the world."[154]

The large ceremonial gatherings in Prairie City during California's centennial year of 1950 and in Mormon Island and Negro Hill just prior to the flooding of Folsom Lake in 1953 offer a resounding testament to the vivacity of these communities. The tone of these events extends beyond mere nostalgia into a measure of profound regret. The towns possessed seemingly durable institutions after all: permanent buildings (some of which were extravagantly built), banks and post offices. Each town had its own school. Reverend Baucher, a Methodist minister, ran a circuit each week during the early 1850s, preaching at the churches of Prairie City on Sunday mornings and Mormon Island in the afternoon, as well as the predominantly African American congregation in Negro Hill during the evening.[155]

Prairie City suffered from unenviable geography, as it was positioned halfway between the Sacramento-Placerville Road to the south and the Coloma Road to the north. Conversely, the twin communities of Mormon Island and Negro Hill enjoyed superior locales. In January 1862, ironically just before a great flood engulfed the region, James Hutchings published a glowing review of the Mormon Island–Negro Hill bridge in his *California Magazine*. On his way to the newly discovered Alabaster Caves on the north fork of the American near Wild Goose Flat, he noted, "Leaving Mormon Island we crossed the South Fork of the American River to Negro Hill on a well-built suspension bridge."[156] Private interests maintained the toll bridge well into the 1880s before turning it over to the public, and even after failing five separate times over the century, residents in 1907 successfully petitioned Sacramento County to rebuild the span one last time. One of the Sacramento region's most enduring structures—dating back to 1851—was finally scrapped in favor of Folsom Dam in 1953.[157]

The nineteenth-century residents of these mining communities could scarcely have understood the nostalgia of these 1950s remembrances. Their descendants, living in the midst of a post–World War II economic expansion, with its burgeoning middle class, enjoyed a perspective of economic diversity. They could envision a community adapting to fundamental economic conditions, perhaps developing an industry of recreation and ecotourism out of Hutchings's observations. Only in recent decades could the residents of America's Rust Belt cities have fathomed, at least on some level, the demise of these nineteenth-century mining towns.

At first, the gold strikes hinted at a more equitable distribution of wealth. The gold rush presented enslaved African Americans "an opportunity for the purchase of one's freedom through hard work or an arranged emancipation agreement with their owners."[158] Many were able to accomplish this task within a short time. Reverend Darius Stokes, an African Methodist Episcopal minister in San Francisco during the 1850s, reported that Black miners working in California's gold fields "were able to send over $750,000 back to the South for the purchase of their own freedom or those of family members."[159]

Such rare triumphs evaporated in the wind. Discriminatory laws and their corresponding racial violence hampered wealth accumulation for African American as well as Chinese American communities. Rampant inflation, colloquially referred to as "gouging" or "mining the miners," added another immediate macroeconomic hurdle. Thomas Larkin, the U.S. consul general, upon his visit to Mormon Island in early 1848, informed the miners that "gold rockers were going for $150 in Monterey."[160] Rinaldo Taylor, the general manager of Mormon Island's Tent Store, pointed out that most of these men traveled back home "breaking even at best." Others left with "less than when they arrived."[161] The retrospective mythology of newfound wealth or an expanding middle class was nary a notion for the residents of Mormon Island, Negro Hill and Prairie City, the yawning chasm of inequality a defining feature of the Victorian era.

Instead, these towns embodied the characteristics of a nineteenth-century American company town that typically revolved around extractive

GOOD NEWS

FOR

MINERS.

NEW GOODS,

PROVISIONS, TOOLS,

CLOTHING, &c. &c.

GREAT BARGAINS!

JUST RECEIVED BY THE SUBSCRIBERS, AT THE LARGE TENT ON THE HILL,

A superior Lot of New, Valuable and most DESIRABLE GOODS for Miners and for residents also. Among them are the following:

STAPLE PROVISIONS AND STORES.

Pork, Flour, Bread, Beef, Hams, Mackerel, Sugar, Molasses, Coffee, Teas, Butter & Cheese, Pickles, Beans, Peas, Rice, Chocolate, Spices, Salt, Soap, Vinegar, &c.

EXTRA PROVISIONS AND STORES.

Every variety of Preserved Meats and Vegetables and Fruits, [more than eighty different kinds.] Tongues and Sounds; Smoked Halibut; Dry Cod Fish; Eggs fresh and fine; Figs, Raisins, Almonds and Nuts; China Preserves; China Bread and Cakes; Butter Crackers, Boston Crackers, and many other very desirable and *choice bits.*

DESIRABLE GOODS FOR COMFORT AND HEALTH.

Patent Cot Bedsteads, Mattresses and Pillows, Blankets and Comforters. Also, in Clothing—Overcoats, Jackets, Miner's heavy Velvet Coats and Pantaloons, Woolen Pants, Guernsey Frocks, Flannel Shirts and Drawers, Stockings and Socks, Boots, Shoes; Rubber Waders, Coats, Blankets, &c.

MINING TOOLS, &c.; BUILDING MATERIALS, &c.

Cradles, Shovels, Spades, Hoes, Picks, Axes, Hatchets, Hammers; every variety of Workman's Tools, Nails, Screws, Brads, &c.

SUPERIOR GOLD SCALES.   MEDICINE CHESTS, &c.

Superior Medicine Chests, well assorted, together with the principal Important Medicines for Dysentery, Fever and Fever and Ague, Scurvy, &c.

N.B.—Important Express Arrangement for Miners.

The Subscribers will run an EXPRESS to and from every Steamer, carrying and returning Letters for the Post Office and Expresses to the States. Also, conveying "*GOLD DUST*" or Parcels, to and from the Mines to the Banking Houses, or the several Expresses for the States, insuring their safety——The various *NEWSPAPERS*, from the Eastern, Western and Southern States, will also be found on sale at our stores, together with a large stock of *BOOKS* and *PAMPHLETS* constantly on hand.

Excelsior Tent, Mormon Island,
January 1, 1850.   ALTA CALIFORNIA PRESS.

WARREN & CO.

An advertisement for the Tent Store. *CSP.*

88

industries. The Natoma Water and Mining Company had overwhelming influence over Prairie City, its delivery of water in 1853 serving as the town's foundation and fueling its subsequent expansion. By the end of the century, the company exerted greater control of the mining district, which included providing room and board to its laborers.[162]

Nevertheless, these mining communities did not share the paternalistic and highly orchestrated attributes of Pullman, a city located outside of Chicago in which every aspect of daily life was under the control of a single corporation.[163] Instead, Prairie City, Mormon Island and Negro Hill are best defined as "improvised" company towns. Thus, a better comparison lies with the "unplanned" coal mining community of Summit Hill, Pennsylvania, which fell under the indirect control of the Lehigh Navigation and Mining Company.

A small oligarchy of capitalists controlled economic affairs. Many were attorneys, Amos Catlin a prime example, who incorporated personal resources with legal wherewithal to take advantage of a nascent California legal system. John Plimpton, the late California State Parks historian, observed a typical "build first, get permit later" approach.[164] The Mormon Island–Negro Hill ferry and bridge were examples of this methodology. Sam Brannan quickly built his general store in Mormon Island just after doing the same in Coloma. Rufus Caldwell propped up the Blue Tent, with Dallas Kneass constructing the Miners Hotel shortly thereafter. In Negro Hill, DeWitt Stanford, Leland Stanford's younger brother, built his general supply market, just as Benjamin Parke Avery constructed a drugstore. All capitalized on an ingratiating and fledgling state and local government.[165]

As Mormon Island and Negro Hill reached a zenith in 1852 and 1853, some perceived a direct threat to Sacramento. In the winter of that year, "There was considerable talk about building a railroad line from Sacramento to Mormon Island."[166] Such a rail line made sense. Negro Bar and Granite City (Folsom) were relative backwaters at this time, while Mormon Island, with its toll bridge to Negro Hill, provided a pathway for the El Dorado Turnpike Company to ship goods efficiently along the peninsula to the upper mines.[167]

Unsurprisingly, the teamsters offered vociferous opposition. In a letter written for the *Sacramento Union*, one of them observed:

I notice by the morning papers that there is a project on foot for a Railroad from this city to Mormon Island....But how will it affect this city? I will tell you what the result will be. Sacramento will be reduced to a mere warehouse, a place of transshipment of goods and passengers; a few large hotels and a few warehouses (owned by the company), will be all that will be required.…We have now a specimen of a small scale on the result of suspended teaming. Goods are transported on small steamers up the American River to Hoboken. Nine-tenths of the buildings in this city would be deserted within three months if this state of things should continue; and such in my opinion would be the necessary result of a Railroad to Mormon Island.[168]

The proposed link to Mormon Island does not appear to have been a particularly serious effort. In retrospect, the teamsters' concerns were misplaced, as the Sacramento Valley Railroad proved beneficial to both Folsom and Sacramento.

As for the decline of the mining towns in the late 1850s and early 1860s, conventional historiography offers a compelling but inadequate solution. As surface gold disappeared, increasingly complex mining techniques took the pan and rocker away from the prospector. Industrial mining swept over Prairie City, and later, the thirst for water ultimately overtook Mormon Island and Negro Hill.

The completion of the Sacramento Valley Railroad in 1856, with its terminus first in Negro Bar—renamed Folsom shortly thereafter—coupled with the relocation of the El Dorado county seat from Coloma to Placerville in 1857, shifted the center of gravity to the south and east.

The catastrophic fire of June 1856 that destroyed half of the main plaza in Mormon Island added impetus to the decline. Racial violence, including the murder of Henry Bell, forced some African American residents of Negro Hill to flee to the relative safety of the abolitionist stronghold of Massachusetts Flat one mile upstream on the north fork side of the peninsula.[169] By the early 1860s, a population that once numbered in the thousands had dwindled to a few dozen.[170]

Members of the capitalist power elite went their separate ways. Some left the region and headed back home. Dallas Kneass, the owner of the Miners Hotel, returned to Baltimore. The whereabouts of John Shaw, who constructed the Mormon Island–Negro Hill bridge, remain a mystery, although it is most likely that he ventured back to his native state of Missouri.[171] Benjamin Parke Avery later became President Grant's ambassador to China.[172]

A dispirited Rinaldo Taylor went back home to Massachusetts in the late fall of 1849, just weeks before the Christmas Eve Ball at the Blue Tent

Hotel, a soiree that featured a fiddler playing a violin with a broken string, a daisy-chain of gas lamps above a dirt floor and the requisite stash of whiskey as lonely men arrived from throughout the region, just for a taste of human interaction.[173]

Others made their way to Sacramento. Sam Branann left Mormon Island to focus on his businesses in Sacramento and San Francisco as his Mormon brethren embarked wholesale for Salt Lake in 1848 and 1849. James Warren, the owner of the Tent Store and an amateur botanist whom Taylor deemed a terrible boss, established a hardware store in Sacramento. He later cofounded the California State Fair and introduced the camellia as the Sacramento City Flower. Amos Catlin joined the state legislature and the Board of Equalization before settling into his law practice.[174]

A few of the elite, some of whom were European immigrants who added a cosmopolitan flair, remained in the region and formed a landed gentry. Three families established large nearby wineries. Henry Mette and his family founded the Red Bank operation. The Hart brothers, who emigrated from Rotterdam, owned a small vineyard adjacent to Mormon Island. Benjamin Bugbey ran his Natoma winery farther upstream, closer to Salmon Falls.[175]

Some oversaw rangeland while their neighbors dabbled in viticulture. John Bennett kept a herd of cattle even as he climbed the hierarchy of the Natoma Company. The Darrington brothers, who arrived from England, maintained a ranch on the peninsula. Their numerous descendants attended Negro Hill School long after African Americans departed the town. The Pilliken family from Scotland grazed sheep there well into the twentieth century.[176]

As for the numerous miners and laborers in the area, many left for the gold strikes in British Columbia. Some African Americans joined the effort, while others settled in nearby population centers such as Sacramento, Stockton, San Francisco and Marysville.[177]

Many Chinese Americans remained in the region. Tang, an intrepid miner, gained local fame by employing his pan and rocker at Mormon Island well into the 1880s.[178] Meanwhile, numerous of his Chinese brethren found work in local vineyards, employing their skills as master gardeners. In addition, employee rosters of the Natoma Company indicate increasing majorities of Chinese laborers as the nineteenth century ended.[179] Just as the Chinese Americans built the railroads, they also played a dominant role in building the water infrastructure of the Sacramento region. Long after the town's disappearance, archaeologists have uncovered Chinese artifacts in the Prairie City region, further highlighting their work on the aqueducts and in the mines.[180]

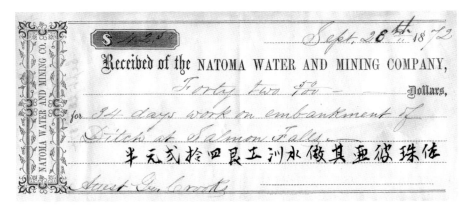

Top: An 1872 pay receipt for a Chinese American laborer from the Natoma Mining and Water Company. *CSP.*

Bottom: Darius King owned a barbershop and bookstore adjacent to the Miner's Hotel. He later owned the Iron Side building on the plaza. *CSP.*

Other groups challenged the dominant social order. For a short time in the spring of 1848, Mormon families resided in Mormon Island, a fleeting counterbalance to the typical male/female ratio of nine to one in the early days of the gold rush.[181] The African American entrepreneurs of the area, most prominently Darius King, who owned no fewer than three businesses and two buildings on the northern plaza of Mormon Island, pointed to a vibrant Black community.

IN DEATH AS IN LIFE

In 1919, the Dutch historian Johann Huizinga revolutionized historiography with *The Waning of the Middle Ages*. In this masterpiece, Huizinga offers a work of historical analysis primarily derived from the interpretation of medieval art and its symbols. The mid-twentieth-century French *Annales* school of historiography ran with Huizenga's breakthrough, promoting the concept of "total history." Instead of biography, as well as political and diplomatic narrative, scholars such as Fernand Braudel and Michel Foucault turned their focus to analytic productions ranging from geography and commerce to social movements and ideology. A pertinent example for our current topic is *Montaillou* by Emanuel Le Roy Ladurie, which examined a small village in the Pyrenees at the center of the Cathar heresy during the Inquisition. In his comprehensive microhistory, Ladurie analyzed, among other things, the burial practices of the townsfolk. In similar fashion, the historian can glean perspective from the cemeteries of Mormon Island, Negro Hill and Prairie City.

In the midst of the Industrial Revolution, people of the Victorian era viewed the home as a sanctuary "ruled by women, where men who toiled in a competitive, unchristian economic sphere could be made civilized, and where children were nurtured."[182] Rinaldo Taylor sheds light on this harsh external world. In his memoirs from 1848 and 1849, Taylor lamented the "loneliness" and "sickness" that plagued the miners, many of whom died "unwept and unmourned."[183] That the first cemetery was consecrated in Mormon Island along the banks of the American during the spring of 1850—a full two years after the settlement of the town—adds a macabre element to his observations. The cemetery was relocated in 1856, partially due to the threat of flooding but mostly because its location was viewed as a superior mining location. There the cemetery resided quietly for nearly another century.[184]

Local cemeteries not only offered visual hallmarks of the Romantic era but also provided a guide to the town's social hierarchy. John Bennett, the Londoner who served as the vice-president of the Natoma Company, has enjoyed the largest monument at the cemetery since his death in 1879. Decorative wrought-iron fences, which were characteristic of the period, surrounded the plots of Bennett and other prominent citizens, although most of the fencing did not survive the 1954 relocation to the present cemetery.[185]

The dozen Prairie City residents exhumed during the Prairie City Road–Highway 50 interchange construction in 1989 were relocated to the current

A 1950 view of the original site of the Mormon Island cemetery, 1850–56. Duncan McCall was the first to be interred there. *CSP.*

Mormon Island cemetery—now located east of Green Valley Road near Mormon Point—after pathologists and anthropologists released their remains in 1994.[186] Over the decades, elements of the Prairie City cemetery had disappeared—headstones and markers were either buried or stolen, with some pieces later found in the backyards of local residents repurposed as landscape ornaments.[187]

Archaeologists, however, recovered enough fragments to discern visual features. The burial plots were decidedly less ornate in comparison to their Mormon Island counterparts, which reflected the relative social standing of the deceased. Although the coffins were simple pine boxes that had badly decomposed, scientists found that one of them, which contained one of the five children interred at the site, was painted in a rose hue, a color

A general view from 1950 of the second Mormon Island cemetery, 1856–1954. *CSP.*

Note the wrought-iron fencing surrounding the plots, a common Romantic era motif. Most of the fencing did not transfer to the current cemetery. *CSP.*

symbolizing the tragic loss of a child. Even though the headstones were too fragmented to provide identification, archaeologists managed to discern an image of a weeping willow on one headstone, an excellent example of naturalistic Romantic iconography.[188]

The cultural practices of Chinese Americans afforded them an escape from the indignities that befell their deceased neighbors. After a period of time, families exhumed the bones of their dead relatives in order to send them back for proper burial in their ancestral homeland.[189]

There was at least one notable exception. The headstone of Chan Lin Din was discovered at the junction of New York Ravine and the south fork of the American River in the early 1950s. According to a translation of his marker, Chan hailed from the village of Hoi Hai in the Sun Wai region of China. His burial plot was transferred in 1954 to the Mormon Island cemetery, where he rests to this day.[190]

The disposition of the cemeteries also provides a stark reminder of racial inequities. On June 2, 1850, Duncan McCall, a medical doctor from Choctaw County Alabama, died of pneumonia. Dr. McCall was the first person laid to rest at the Mormon Island cemetery, "interred in a grave hewn by rock."[191]

Duncan McCall arrived at Mormon Island in 1849 accompanied by his brother Daniel, by way of New Orleans and the isthmus of Panama. Daniel McCall, also a medical doctor, welcomed their other brother, Charlie, in 1851. After spending some time mining along the banks of Mormon Island, the McCall brothers established a mining operation a mile south at Beam's Bar, which was adjacent to the Nuttall property, now the site of Folsom Prison.[192]

Although Charlie McCall returned to Alabama in 1855, with Daniel holding out until 1857, they both maintained economic interests in the region; one real estate transaction from 1858 indicated co-ownership of a farm in Brighton.[193] Daniel McCall would later serve as a surgeon in the Confederate army during the Civil War, after which he practiced medicine

The McCall brothers' Beam's Bar operation in 1856. *CSP.*

The original site of Negro Hill cemetery, seen in 1952. *CSP*

in Choctaw County Alabama until his death in 1897. Charlie McCall, who was injured in the Battle of Bentonville, later became a prominent lawyer in Alabama, a fact that would later ensure the successful relocation of the Mormon Island cemetery upon construction of Folsom Dam.[194]

On October 11, 1945, and with a new reservoir on the horizon, Governor Earl Warren and his staff extended the courtesy of notifying Alabama Governor Chauncey Sparks about the imminent repatriation of their native son. As it turned out, staff in Montgomery knew exactly who to contact. Over the next twenty years, a remarkable flurry of correspondence whistled between Montgomery, Mobile and Sacramento.[195]

Charles McCall, the grandson of Daniel McCall and grand-nephew of Duncan McCall, ran a prominent legal practice in Mobile. In the 1960s, Charles McCall was appointed to the Nineteenth Circuit of the state court, but before that event, he used his stature in Alabama circles to ensure the proper relocation of the cemetery that contained the remains of his grand-uncle. After the successful repatriation in 1954, McCall would continue his correspondence, this time with John Plimpton, who was, at that time, a deputy superintendent with California State Parks in San Francisco. McCall donated documents and photographs to the state park collection, so much so that his contributions are contained in a separate volume.[196]

Difficult ironies abound. Firstly, there was the correspondence between Governor Earl Warren, who on one hand authored *Brown v. Board of Education* yet was complicit in the internment of Japanese Americans, and

98

Governor Chauncey Sparks, an arch-segregationist and mentor to George Wallace. And then there were the two surviving McCall brothers, soldiers in the Confederate army who served in rebellion against the United States.

Meanwhile, the transferred remains of the thirty-six people from Negro Hill, all unidentified, suffered for more than a half-century under markers desecrated by the racial slur as their place name. Only in 2011, due to the hard work of activists, was this racist neglect remedied with new plates.[197]

A Striking Evolution

Occasionally, a member of the elite challenges the status quo, which brings forth the curious case of Benjamin Bugbey. Until recent years, local historians have painted a caricature of Bugbey. The macabre death of his wife, Mary Jane, in 1869 and his drunken revelry, replete with state fair medals and his "Champagne waltz and gallop," have been material for bar room trivia and ghost tours. Yet Bugbey's life, particularly his later years, offers a complex and compelling portrait.

Bugbey's Natoma Winery slowly deteriorated after its apex in the early 1870s, finally entering bankruptcy and foreclosure in 1877. A number of reasons contributed to its demise, which included a national grape glut caused by a deep recession in the mid-1870s.[198] Coupled with ongoing legal battles versus the Natoma Company and the influence of his late father, a Methodist/Episcopalian minister, Bugbey underwent a change in his worldview.[199]

A radical transformation ensued. On one front, Bugbey's views on Chinese Americans evolved in a similar fashion to Mark Twain's attitudes toward Native Americans. At first, he tested the patience of local citizens even as they were imbued with anti-Chinese prejudice. Under Bugbey's leadership as Sacramento sheriff in 1862, his deputies detained Chew Yew and tortured him at police headquarters. *Sacramento Union* reporters, whose office shared a wall with the police station, heard the commotion and promptly recorded the incident in the following day's edition. At best, as the journalists surmised, Bugbey lacked control over his deputies. The scandal contributed to Bugbey's defeat upon reelection, losing to his former friend James McClatchy.[200]

Later in the decade, however, Bugbey would employ an estimable cadre of Chinese American agronomists at his Natoma Winery. This was not remarkable in and of itself, as the Red Bank winery also employed its own phalanx of Chinese American specialists, as did other entities. But Bugbey stood out by frequently describing "his Chinese employees as loyal and hardworking."[201] More striking, however, was his real estate deal with Mum Sing of Folsom. Selling property to a Chinese American family violated a taboo of the time.[202]

His actions as U.S. marshal in the late 1880s present the most captivating evidence of his transformation. The late nineteenth and early twentieth centuries were a particularly difficult era for Asian Americans, and the decade of the 1880s was an exceptionally perilous time for Chinese Americans. With the Chinese Exclusion Act of 1882, signed by President Chester A. Arthur as the backdrop, anti-Chinese clubs, essentially vigilante groups, terrorized immigrant communities. Employing intimidation and outright physical violence, these mobs sought to evict Chinese American families from their neighborhoods.

Bugbey, who was appointed to his position by President Arthur, attempted a daring prosecution. A group of sixteen White vigilantes was arrested in the farming town of Nicolaus, which is located about twenty miles north of Sacramento. The anti-Chinese throng donned masks "and descended on the hop fields around Nicolaus and drove 46 Chinese workers off their property and loaded them on a barge on the river."[203]

With the Burlingame Treaty as its foundation, along with citations from the 1866 Civil Rights Act and section 5519 of the United States Code, Bugbey and his fellow prosecutors secured a victory at the federal circuit court. Bugbey's friend Lorenzo Sawyer, a former California Supreme Court justice, was the presiding federal judge and issued the majority ruling. Dissenting justices, however, triggered a review by the U.S. Supreme Court.[204]

While noting the egregiousness of the incident, the U.S. Supreme Court nonetheless ruled in favor of the defense. Chinese Americans did not warrant federal protection.[205]

Bugbey and his prosecutors were ahead of their time. In effect, their arguments presaged the section of the 1964 Civil Rights Act that contains the principle of protected classes. In a rebuke, his Republican counterparts introduced a plank on the party platform calling for the repeal of the Burlingame Treaty.[206]

Benjamin Bugbey's political beliefs underwent a concurrent transformation. Borrowing from scripture, specifically from the Old Testament book of Leviticus, he championed a utopian vision that encapsulated his Progressive era ideology. Perhaps influenced by the utopian communities of Brook Farm and Oneida, he proposed a Jubilee system of government that called for periodic cancelation of debt and land redistribution.[207]

His ideology nonetheless belied a practical program for action. Bugbey championed the economic principles of Henry George.[208] George's views on land reform and taxation, most particularly his land tax, remain influential with the New Keynsian economists such as Nobel laureates Paul Krugman and Joseph Stiglitz.[209]

Bugbey's views of a disintegrating society corresponded with the deterioration of the natural environment. An inhabitant a mere two centuries ago would scarcely recognize the current landscape. Riparian forests, which stretched for miles from each riverbank, are now restricted to narrow channels. Oak woodlands have vastly shrunk. Wildflowers, as well as native bunch grasses, once blanketed the Central Valley, offering the traveler an experience John Muir once described as "walking on liquid gold."[210] Now the carpet of endemic blooms, along with 90 percent of the Central Valley's vernal pool habitat, has largely disappeared.[211] By the late nineteenth century, dams, diversions and hydraulic mining eliminated, in entirety, the salmon run along the lower American River.[212] The chaparral ecosystem near historic Mormon Island, its gabbroic and serpentine soils home to a stunning 10 percent of California's endemic plants, remains resilient though fractured by development.[213]

As with the environment, the towns of Mormon Island, Negro Hill and Prairie City suffered from neglect, dismissal, even destruction. Bugbey's disillusionment and radicalism points to the inherent stratified class structure of nineteenth-century California. People in these towns, fractious as they were, sought a measure of permanence. Instead, they remained ephemeral, made expendable by a capitalist elite.

CHAPTER 6

MORMON ISLAND

By Eric Webb

CONFIDENCE BETRAYED

A common theme in the early days of the California Gold Rush were the numerous, yet futile, attempts to keep secret news of the first gold discoveries. In June 1848, the United States consul in Monterey, Thomas Larkin, after his return from the gold fields, quickly sent a message to Secretary of State James Buchanan in Washington, D.C. In a reference to the gold strike at Coloma, Larkin asserted that "the discovery was made by some Mormons in January or February who for a time kept it secret."[214] Larkin may have been referring to the half-dozen members of the disbanded Mormon Battalion who were fellow employees of James Marshall and were present in Coloma. But it was, in fact, Johann Sutter and Marshall who tried to keep a lid on the affair. "While at Coloma Sutter urged secrecy upon his employees."[215]

The surreptitiousness became contagious. While honoring their contract with Sutter and his sawmill, the Battalion Boys searched for gold during odd hours and off-days. Henry Bigler, one of the Battalion members who kept a journal of events, traveled a half-mile downstream under the guise of a deer hunt on February 6. He subsequently returned to his secret mining activities on February 15 and February 20, securing a nifty "$24 in gold dust when wages were a mere $1.50 per day."[216]

Many of Bigler's comrades toiled at Sutter's gristmill, located in an area that soon became the town of Brighton. Perhaps feeling a tinge of guilt,

Bigler sent a note on his findings to his mates at the mill. He implored them "to keep it to themselves unless it would be someone who could keep a secret. Mr. Marshall did not want it to be known until further development."[217]

Intrigued by Bigler's message, three men from the Battalion set foot on the Coloma Road from Sutter's gristmill. On February 27, Sidney Willis, Wilford Hudson and Levi Fifield arrived in Coloma, where they found a loquacious James Marshall sharing stories about the gold discovery.[218] Sam Brannan, the appointed leader of the Battalion and California's Mormon community, caught word of the activity and immediately leased a building from Sutter, opening a general store in Coloma in anticipation of the impending stampede.[219]

On March 2, 1848, Hudson, Willis, Bigler and Fifield left Coloma to return to the Natoma mill. However, while Fifield and Bigler traveled in normal fashion by way of the Coloma Road, Willis and Hudson embarked westward along the banks of the south fork of the American River. In the late afternoon, they came upon an oxbow about one mile upstream from the confluence with the north fork, twenty-five miles northeast of Sacramento almost precisely midway to Coloma.[220]

Prior to Willis and Hudson's arrival, Jedediah Smith, his African American partner Peter Ranne and their entourage most likely set up camp at or near this location for a week or two in May 1827 as they awaited the flooded American River to recede. On March 4, 1844, Captain John C. Frémont came upon the Mormon Island site as he traversed down the south fork of the American on his journey from Oregon to Sutter's Fort via the Carson River to the east. Other than those two occurrences, the Valley Nisenan, over the millennia, were the only people to see or occupy this location. Indeed, the advantageous environs of the surrounding area indicate the likelihood of a Nisenan village.[221]

Willis and Hudson believed that they encountered a mirage, finding only a few specks of gold after seeing a noticeable glint in the distance. They paid little mind to their discovery and kept on their journey to the Natoma gristmill. When the two men showed Bigler the gold they had found at their site, he agreed with their initial assessment: "I saw the particles and passed my judgment that there was not to exceed fifty cents worth of very fine particles, so trifling a prospect in our estimation that they had no notion of examining it any further." But two other Battalion comrades, Ephraim Green and Ira Willis, Sidney's brother, encouraged them to return to the site.[222]

On April 8, Bigler and Fifield arrived at the Natoma mill after a trip from Coloma and a quick stop at Sutter's Fort. Bigler found that several of

The original site of Willis and Hudson's March 1848 discovery as seen in 1930. The Hoxsie chicken ranch is in the background. *CSP.*

their workmates had ventured upriver "getting gold and had been for several days, but how they were making it no one seemed to know." Bigler and a few of his men headed up toward Coloma and, after an overnight stay in the riparian wilderness, came upon seven Battalion Boys working the river at the new site. The seven men made $250 in one day at the very place Hudson and Willis camped in early March. The men used Native American–made baskets, washing out gold to the tune of $0.25 to $2 per load.[223]

In the meantime, one or both of the Willis brothers had set out for Yerba Buena (San Francisco) to notify Sam Brannan of their discovery at Mormon Island. Brannan immediately promised them, deceptively, that he would secure the land title for the church. He imposed a 30 percent tithe or tax, with 10 percent for the title, another 10 percent for a temple that he promised to build in California and a final 10 percent for regular tithing.[224] Brannan kept the proceeds; the tax never funded any of its intended purposes.

As Brannan put the squeeze on his followers, the gold discoveries at Coloma and Mormon Island simultaneously tightened Sutter's purse strings. A number of the Natoma gristmill workers, as well as the laborers at the sawmill, found regular and back pay withheld. One of the Battalion members, James S. Brown, complained that he received "nary a farthing for one hundred days work." In retrospect, Brown offered up a more charitable view of Sutter and Marshall: "People took advantage of them. Every other enterprise was sacrificed in the rush for gold." Sutter was about to be overrun, and Brannan was a gleeful participant.[225]

Brannan's own attempt to keep the gold discovery under wraps soon unraveled. On March 15, 1848, the *Californian* newspaper broke the news in San Francisco: "Gold Mine Found—In the newly made raceway of the saw mill recently erected by Captain Sutter on the American Fork, gold has been found in considerable quantities."[226]

Sure enough, Brannan was compelled to address the discovery three days later on March 18 in his rival San Francisco paper, the *California Star*. The editors struck a self-interested tone: "Gold-the veritable gold, itself has been dragged forth, and now that it has been turned from the earth without sowing, we wouldn't be willing to make a prediction where the excitement caused will cease."[227]

Brannan had actually "scooped" his rivals at the *Californian*, and the subsequent tone of the *Star*'s reporting lent credence to Larkin's assertions to Buchanan. Brannan certainly had incentive to delay as much as possible— more time to collect the 30 percent tax on his miners and enough leeway to establish storefronts in both Coloma and Mormon Island.

Nevertheless, Larkin's missive to Buchanan lacked context even if not downright incorrect. Brannan and the Battalion Boys merely did at Mormon Island what Marshall and Sutter did at Coloma. Their secrets were short-lived, as both the *Star* and *Californian* added entries to the narrative in April and May 1848. It was around this time in early May that Sam Brannan made his legendary exhortation in the streets of San Francisco. Swinging a vial of gold dust, he shouted, "Gold! Gold! Gold in the American River!"[228]

While his exhortation is fodder for modern-day legend, the people of San Francisco must have viewed Brannan's outburst with a measure of befuddlement as well as seeing it as incredibly self-serving. A multitude of prospectors had been mining the American River for months. An exodus from San Francisco was already in full gear, so much so that the *Californian* suspended publication on May 21, and the *California Star* followed suit on June 11.[229]

On April 1, 1848, the *Star* published a special edition detailing California's newfound "mineral wealth."[230] Copies were shipped back east overland and by ship.[231] On April 19, the *Californian* reported, "It is stated that a new mine has been discovered on the American Fork of the Sacramento supposed to be on the land of W.A. Leidesdorff Esq."[232] This was most likely a reference to the strike at Negro Bar (across the river from the current state park at Black Miner's Bar) just southwest of Mormon Island. Likewise, on April 22, the *Star* reported on another gold mine, this time upstream from Mormon Island. "We have been informed from unquestionable authority that another still more extensive and valuable gold mine has been discovered towards the head of the American Fork in the Sacramento Valley."[233] In this case, the reporting most assuredly was in reference to a strike near Salmon Falls.[234]

Back at Mormon Island, one of the Battalion members, Azariah Smith, noted on April 23, 1848, "Before we came away, men, women and children, from the Bay and other places in California, were flocking to the gold mine, by the dozens and by wagon loads." Smith also offered a representative take on the early days at Mormon Island: "The most I made in a day was sixty-five dollars after the toll was taken out, which was thirty dollars out of a hundred which goes to Hudson and Willis that discovered the mine and Brannan who is securing it for them."[235]

On May 5, after departing from Sutter's Fort, Brannan and his business partner, Charles C. Smith, made their first visit to Mormon Island. Upon their arrival, they "found the island with just a shallow stream dividing it from the mainland, which would be just another river bar when the river dropped a few weeks later." Eventually, this "high water stream" on the backside of the oxbow would be repurposed as a canal.[236]

Brannan observed fifty men at work on the river, at this point a bare majority of them Mormon, as daily wagon trains made their arrival. On June 27, 1848, a survey of inhabitants listed twenty-seven members of the erstwhile Mormon Battalion working the mine at Mormon Island. They claimed to have cleared one hundred pounds of gold in their first thirty days, measured and sorted in pint and half-pint containers.[237]

Another Battalion member, Alexander Stephens, engineered what may have been the original rocker of the California Gold Rush. He hollowed out a wooden trough with a round bottom. He rocked the sand and gravel back and forth, forcing the gold to settle at the bottom. He refined his invention by securing the trough "on an incline so that the gold would work down to the lower end."[238] Stephens's innovation was undoubtedly more valuable than any gold he could have prospected. But he was disinclined to sequester his invention, especially from his Mormon brethren, and in any case had little wherewithal to file a patent.

A number of luminaries arrived at Mormon Island in the months of June and July 1848. John Bidwell stopped to survey the scene on his way up to Coloma. An eighteen-year-old John Breen, whose family came with the Donner Party from Iowa, scoured the banks of the burgeoning township before heading for Placerville in the fall. James Reed, also of the Donner Party, tried his luck in July. James Lick spent one month in Mormon Island before doubling back to San Francisco. He would amass a real estate empire, deploying his wealth to fund the astronomy department at the University of California and its observatory on Mount Hamilton.[239]

A day after Independence Day celebrations at Sutter's Fort, the military governor, U.S. Army General James Mason, Second Lieutenant William T. Sherman and Quartermaster Joseph Folsom, Mason's African American servant and four other soldiers arrived at Mormon Island. This was their first stop on an official inspection of the gold fields. In a letter sent to Brigadier General Jones back in Washington, D.C., Mason reported:

> *I resumed my journey twenty-five miles up the American Fork-from Sutter's Fort where they had celebrated the Fourth of July-to a point now known as the "lower mines" or "Mormon Diggings." The hillsides were thickly strewn with canvas tents and brush arbors, a store (Sam Brannan's) was erected and several boarding shanties were in operation. The day was intensely hot yet about two hundred men were at work in the full glare of the sun, washing for gold; some with tin pans, and some with close-woven Indian baskets, but the greatest part had rude machines, known as the cradle.*[240]

Mason also heard the complaints about Brannan's mining tax. With a sniff of condescension, Mason surmised, "That Brannan had a perfect right to collect for as long as they were foolish enough to pay it." Mason and his entourage soon left for Coloma but made a return visit on July 8 as they headed back to Sutter's Fort, San Francisco and Monterey.[241]

The northeastern side of the Mormon Island Plaza circa 1853. *SCP.*

A drawing of the Townshend Ranch in the early 1850s. *CSP.*

Mormon settlers left en masse shortly after Mason's visit. They sought to catch up with Henry Bigler and his train of seventeen wagons that had departed Pleasant Valley, near Placerville, on July 4 for Salt Lake. Although Bigler's company was originally slated to leave on June 1, heavy snowfall from the previous winter and the attractive windfall from the gold fields delayed the journey. The migrants pioneered a road from Pleasant Valley through Carson Valley on their way east. Fortified with numerous copies of Brannan's April 1 special edition of the *California Star*, they arrived in Salt Lake in October 1848.

Although it is not clear how many Mormons remained in the new township after the 1848 exodus, enough remained in Mormon Island to justify Brannan's tax. However, after another mass exit in the summer of 1849, only a handful of Mormons remained, the vast majority having finally left for Salt Lake. This prompted Brannan's return to Sacramento.[242]

The absence of the Mormon community was more than made up for by a tidal wave of migrants from the United States and abroad. Mormon Island, situated just upstream from the confluence of the north and south forks of the American River, possessed a natural geographic advantage. The town was just one quarter mile off the Coloma Road, from which a

The Townshend Ranch in 1922. *CSP.*

spur into town was quickly developed. It was also twenty-five miles closer to Sutter's Fort than Coloma and soon became a supply center for the many settlements nearby. A ferry over the south fork, supplanted by a bridge, aided in the transport of goods to the sister township of Negro Hill immediately across the way. Materials were then transported up the peninsula by road to such settlements as Rattlesnake Bar, Condemned Bar and Massachusetts Flat.[243]

THE NEW TOWN

When Sam Brannan visited Mormon Island in May 1848, before the Mormon emigration, he scouted a site for a new general store. Brannan selected his *Brooklyn* shipmate William Stout to manage his business. Sutter dispatched three wagons, loaded with dry goods, to Mormon Island on May 19. The next day, two additional wagons were sent to supply Brannan's store in Coloma. Brannan himself arrived at Mormon Island on May 21 "to look after his interests."[244]

Laborers hastily constructed the store at Mormon Island consisting of a log framework and canvas. A "lean-to" was added to the temporary structure in order to provide a ramshackle "hotel."[245] J. Tyrwhite Brooks, who arrived on June 4, 1848, noted Brannan's plans for a permanent structure, referring to him as "a sallow Yankee, the owner of a large heap of planks and framing lumber laying a hundred yards from the river where he was planning to build a store."[246]

Business was strong "even before the final canvas was in place."[247] John Breen offered an insight on Brannan's initial monopoly:

> Sam Brannan had the only store here (at Mormon Island in June of 1848). He must have made a lot of money as there were many people mining and gold was plenty and many bought things that they did not need or sold their gold to Brannan for five or six dollars an ounce, there being reports that the stuff was not gold. Others thought that even if it was gold it would be so abundant that it would be worthless and so they would give it for anything they saw for sale.[248]

As incoming migrants replaced the departed Mormons, the township developed a bustling downtown with three dry goods stores, five general merchandise stores, a blacksmith and butcher shop, a bakery and two livery stables. The Adams Company and Wells Fargo Express offices provided financial services. Perhaps most important to the citizenry, seven saloons quickly began operations. The Jim Birch Company of Sacramento started daily stage line service from Sacramento in September 1849. A stunning success from the beginning, the Jim Birch stage line morphed into the California Stage Company, which became the largest and most estimable operation in the state.[249]

Rufus Caldwell established the first hotel in the fall of 1848. Constructed of ninety poles made of pine covered by blue denim, it accommodated up to forty guests. The hotel came to be known as the perhaps all too obvious "Blue Tent Hotel," although some referred to it as the "Blue Drilling Hotel."

The accommodations, at least initially, were spartan. Occupants slept on the earthen floor, and Caldwell only had two blankets to spare at first. The first two tenants to bed at night would get the blankets, but Caldwell was known to clandestinely take one back for himself after a patron fell asleep. If there was an objection, he would smooth things over by "offering a stiff shot of bourbon and a fifty-cent cigar."[250]

A flurry of opaque transactions occurred in the early days of Mormon Island as a mercantile oligarchy consolidated power. Brannan bought out Charles Smith's interest in the general store at Sutter's Fort. For a time during the halcyon days of 1849, Brannan took an average of $5,000 per day. By the summer of 1849, Brannan had begun to turn his focus away from Mormon Island in favor of his interests in Sacramento and San Francisco.

Brannan put his Natoma Store, as it was now called, up for sale, completing the transaction on August 18, 1849. William Stout was more than pleased to leave his employment at the Natoma Store. Engorged with many months of profits, he sailed back to his native state of Maryland.[251]

The transaction went smoothly. The Connecticut Mining and Trading Company, based in Sacramento and headed by Thomas McDowell, took on the interest from Sam Brannan. The transfer included 205 acres of surrounding land. Of greater importance, a ferry operation was included in the sale. This ferry service connected Mormon Island on the left bank of the South Fork of the American River to its sister township of Negro Hill on the confluence peninsula. The ferry provided an essential piece of infrastructure by connecting people and supplies from the Sacramento-Coloma Road to the burgeoning settlement of Negro Hill and beyond.[252]

McDowell, an attorney who migrated from New Jersey to Sacramento, quickly initiated a series of dizzying and complex real estate transactions. Myriad deeds of trust were recorded in Sacramento in 1850 that ultimately divided the Natoma Store, the ferry operation and the surrounding land in thirds. At various junctures in 1850, entities such as the Phoenix Mining and Trading Company and the Thomas Warbass and Company, which was helmed by John Morse and DeWitt Stanford, signed on with McDowell and the Connecticut Company. Stanford and Morse also bought interests across the way in Negro Hill. McDowell memorialized ferry operations by securing an official license from the newly incorporated Sacramento County in August 1850.[253]

The ferry was a remarkably lucrative enterprise. Tolls began at fifty cents for a single person and quickly increased to one dollar per crossing. A person and their horse cost two dollars at first but increased to three dollars. By the end of the year in 1850, E.S. Woodford of Sacramento, the principal agent of the Phoenix company, managed to acquire the entire operation. In just a few months, Woodford then titled the operation to Amos Catlin.[254]

Catlin's subsequent transactions remain a bit of a mystery. Plimpton summarized the absence of documentation: "Nothing has been found to whom Catlin sold the ferry and little as to the sale and ownership of the rest of the old Sam Brannan holdings at Mormon Island." The last owner of the ferry, emerging from the vortex of transactions, was Dallas Kneass, the owner of the Miners Hotel.[255]

THE PLAZA

Although the canvas tents of prospectors dotted the surrounding landscape, Mormon Island featured a main thoroughfare that widened considerably into a central plaza. This large rectangular plaza consisted of numerous prominent businesses. The land parcels, or plots, surrounding the central district had average dimensions of 50 feet in width and 150 to 160 feet in depth, although there were many notable exceptions. The northern length of the plaza featured a dozen lots, while the southern side had ten. Three lots filled the western end of the plaza, with a ravine serving as the eastern border. Other notable buildings were constructed outside the central district, such as the Hoxsie and Stephenson Houses, farther east of the ravine. The plaza was situated a quarter mile upstream of the ferry and, after 1852, the Shaw bridge. A small hill, or ridgeline, on the back lots of the northern plaza separated the downtown district from the south fork of the American River, where miners worked the sandbars. The central district featured a plethora of enterprises between 1848 and 1856, often changing hands among the capitalist elite of Mormon Island and Sacramento.[256]

The Miners Hotel, later known as the National or Natoma Hotel, was the largest and most prominent landmark in Mormon Island. African American and Chinese American residents built the structure for Dallas Kneass and his partner John Hart in late 1851. The enterprise served guests in a dual capacity, as both a general store and lodge. The store was located on the ground floor, a place where "the miner could buy just about anything he needed, food, clothing, tools and even a drink-by the glass or by the bottle."[257] A boardinghouse occupied the second floor, its rooms rented out as a separate independent business.[258]

The Exchange Hotel anchored the south side of the plaza. It became the most prominent landmark after Rufus Caldwell converted his Blue Tent Hotel into a general store in 1851. John Shaw built the Exchange and then transferred the title outright to Amos Catlin, as indicated by a bill of sale dated June 1, 1852. The Natoma Water and Mining Company was founded, at least in part, at the Exchange.[259]

Financially overextended by his new Natoma Mining and Water Corporation and the construction costs of the Natoma Ditch, Catlin returned to Sacramento in March 1853. He promptly drew up rental papers for the Exchange, leasing the venture to F.E. Mumford.[260]

An 1852 drawing of Mormon Island with the Shaw bridge and Negro Hill in the background. *CSP.*

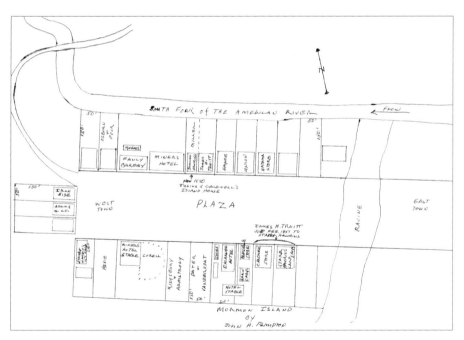

California State Parks historian John Plimpton's map of the Mormon Island Plaza, circa 1855. *CSP.*

The Miners Hotel in 1851. Negro Hill is in the background. *CSP.*

The Exchange Hotel in the 1880s. *CSP.*

In 1854, Catlin used this windfall to fund extensive repairs and improvements to the Exchange Hotel with an eye toward selling the property. While the Miners Hotel was Mormon Island's largest building, Catlin's upgrades rewarded patrons of the Exchange with luxurious accommodations. Valets stabled horses behind the hotel for easy access, while a shoemaker and carpentry shop provided services in adjacent buildings. The hotel itself housed a saloon and bar room on the first floor, with guest rooms occupying both the first and second levels.[261]

In a May 2, 1963 retrospective, the *Orangevale News* extolled the virtues of the Exchange Hotel:

> *The building was erected in 1851, the lumber having been brought here by steamer around the Horn. In those days, when Mormon Island was a lively camp, the hotel was regarded as one of the finest in this part of the state. Many teamsters and miners bound for the mines of El Dorado County found it a favorite stopping place.*[262]

Perhaps sensing a decline in the township's fortunes, coupled with his legal and political ambitions, Catlin sold the property in January 1856.[263]

COMMUNITY

While white Americans and European immigrants are well represented in the historical record, African Americans, Chinese Americans and other groups were typically dismissed and ignored. Voting records are absent due to discrimination, while others were not properly enumerated in the federal census. With a few notable exceptions, many journals and diaries have been lost to time.

Prior to the California Gold Rush, only a handful of African Americans resided in the state, making their way as cooks, trappers and laborers. Some gained a measure of fame, such as Peter Ranne, who accompanied Jedediah Smith to California in 1826; James Beckwourth, who blazed the northern Sierra Nevada trail; and Allen Light, who worked for the Mexican government. Most notable perhaps was William Leidesdorff, who oversaw a cattle empire in Sacramento County on his thirty-five-thousand-acre land grant along the American River.

When news of the gold strikes at Mormon Island and Coloma reached San Francisco in 1848, a stampede of prospectors flocked to the American

River. Some of the first to reach the gold fields were the sailors of New England whaling ships. Most of the vessels employed African American cooks, who accompanied their shipmates in the early rush to the mines.[264]

Although many arrived at Coloma, most descended on the mining sites of Mormon Island, Negro Bar and Negro Hill. In the 1850 census, 962 African Americans were recorded in California, and in 1852, the ranks swelled to well over two thousand. Black miners who initially came to Negro Bar in the early days of 1849 eventually left for better prospects in 1850, many settling in nearby Negro Hill. A second strike at Negro Hill in 1852 reinforced this migration.[265]

Although the census does not indicate the status of African Americans, free or enslaved, recent scholars have approximated their status based on place of birth and the number of Black people in a household.

F. Gray of Maryland and George Brown of Massachusetts, aged thirty-one and thirty, respectively, were listed as laborers. J.W. Pearle, thirty-two, of Pennsylvania and W. Jackson, forty-three, of New York were enumerated as miners. Mary Dell, a twenty-four-year-old from the Sandwich Islands (Hawaii), who was the sole woman of the group, and B. Johnson, thirty-seven, of Nova Scotia, were also recorded as miners. These residents of Mormon Island were most likely free persons. Armstead Clayton, twenty-six, of Virginia; C.G. Howland, thirty-three, of Washington, D.C.; and Mary Litchner, twenty-six, of Kentucky, on the other hand, were most likely enslaved.[266]

Mormon Island was also home to a prominent Black entrepreneur. Darius King operated the Barbershop and Bookstore immediately adjacent to the Miners Hotel. The business was contained in a thirty-by-thirty-foot wood-frame building owned by Samuel Hawkins. King had a flourishing business due to its proximity to the hotel.[267]

Perhaps due to his success with his barbershop and bookstore, King constructed, sometime before 1855, a building on the northwest corner of the plaza at the site of the defunct Adams and Company building. The structure was relatively large, on a lot measuring 50 by 150 feet. It was known as the Iron Side, but the nature of King's business there remains unknown.[268]

Darius King was a contemporary of Edward Duplex, who, like King, owned a barbershop. Duplex oversaw his business in Marysville and gained renown for his hairstyling abilities at the California State Fair in 1858. Duplex was a delegate for Yuba County at the inaugural California Colored Convention, which was held at St. Andrew's AME Church in Sacramento in 1855. Later, in 1888, Duplex was elected mayor of Wheatland, becoming the first African American mayor on the West Coast. It is hard to imagine that Darius King and Edward Duplex were not at least acquaintances, given the prominence and shared interests of both these men.[269]

Women accounted for a mere 10 percent of the population in the early days of the California Gold Rush.[270] However, Mormon Island may have been a bit of an outlier, as a number of Mormon families arrived in 1848. One such family, William and Jane Glover and their two girls and one son, arrived in Yerba Buena (San Francisco) on the *Brooklyn* in 1846. Shortly after their arrival, another son was born, William Francisco. Catching word from their Battalion brethren, the Glovers headed up to Mormon Island in the spring of 1848.[271]

Families encountered challenging conditions. For instance, while her family panned for gold, Jane Glover dug a hole in the sandbar in an effort to secure her infant. The Glovers, along with other Mormon families, subsequently left for Salt Lake in the summer of 1849. But the Glovers' resilience and fortitude paid off, and they embarked with one and a half pecks, or twelve quarts, of gold.[272]

Ella Sterling Mighels in 1890. *CSP.*

Mormon Island produced notable women. A prominent early literary figure of California was Ella Sterling Clark Mighels. Using the pen name "Aurora Esmeralda," Mighels began her writing career in 1869 as a student at Sacramento High School. Over the ensuing decades, she would pen numerous essays, articles and books for a wide array of outlets, including the *Sacramento Union*. In 1918, the California state legislature appointed Mighels as the "first historian of literary California."[273]

Ella Mighels's early life was particularly tragic. Her father, Sterling Clark, died seven months before she was born, leaving her mother, Rachel, widowed and pregnant. In a heartwarming twist, empathetic miners offered a gift for the new mother, a cradle, "but such as one as no other baby ever had before or since. It was a gold rocker, one that had seen hard service washing gold in the American River, now all nicely cleaned and dried, and presented to me for my own."[274]

Rachel Clark remarried Dudley Haskell, who owned the Union Hotel in Mormon Island, a few months after the birth of her daughter. The family ultimately resettled in Sacramento at a home on 8th and N Streets.[275]

Before her relocation to Sacramento, however, Ella Mighels spent time at a new Mormon Island school, which was opened by her mother, Rachel, in 1853, as she saw an increasing influx of women and children who made the town their new home.[276]

In November 1858, a public school took its place. The Natoma Township School Commission placed an advertisement in regional newspapers that sought "a female teacher to teach at Mormon Island school." The salary was forty dollars per month "plus board and room in the home of a good family."[277]

The school burned down in 1887. Classes were temporarily held at the nearby Watt House, which stood adjacent to the Mansion House, or the Stephenson House, as it was called by then. In 1890, a new structure was built, closer to "Blue Ravine near the Hoke property." At this time, the school joined the newly formed Natoma School District and remained in operation until 1953.[278]

Teresa Schone owned and operated one of the most profitable businesses during the post–gold rush era of Mormon Island. Although it is not quite clear when the Schone Saloon exactly sprung into existence, most likely the early 1880s, it enjoyed a number of years as a Mormon Island landmark.

Opposite: The Mormon Island class of 1886–87. The original school burned down shortly thereafter. *FHM.*

Right: The Mormon Island school, seen here in the 1940s, was constructed in 1890. *FHM.*

Below: Theresa Schone's saloon in 1903. *CSP.*

The saloon was located at the junction of Negro Hill and Mormon Island–Folsom Roads, a quarter mile equidistant from the old city plaza to the east and the Mormon Island bridge to the north. Its location ensured success, capturing tourists and locals heading in three directions, either for Folsom, Mormon Island or up the peninsula.[279]

An article from the *Folsom Telegraph* in 1887 raved about the saloon's offerings: "The bowling alley of Mrs. Schone's Saloon, Mormon Island, has just been put in good working order by Mr. Camenzland and is now the best bowling alley in this part of the country. Mrs. Schone has also gotten in a supply of fine wines, liquors, and cigars and prepared to satisfy the most fastidious."[280] Schone would eventually sell the building to Charles Darrington, who operated a ranch near Negro Hill. Sometime in the 1920s, a wildfire destroyed the building. It was never rebuilt.[281]

A Tale of Resilience: The Mormon Island–Negro Hill Ferry and Bridge

Not long after the Willis and Hudson discovery, a road connected Mormon Island with Negro Bar, which was later subsumed by Folsom Lake. This roadway ran parallel to the existing Coloma Road, which traversed roughly along the current-day corridor of Natoma Street and Green Valley Road. The Folsom–Mormon Island Road ran along the south fork of the American River, carving through present-day Folsom Prison and Folsom Dam headlong into the now submerged town. This roadway extended into the plaza district, where it widened considerably, extending for yet another half-mile eastward before reconnecting with the Coloma Road. About one half-mile in the opposite direction downriver from the Mormon Island central plaza, a quarter-mile spur connected the roadway to the ferry terminal on the south fork of the American.[282]

Beginning in 1849, a number of stage lines provided daily round-trip service between Mormon Island and Sacramento. Other lines soon joined the lucrative enterprise, including the Joseph Gregory Company in 1850 and the Hunter and Adams lines in 1852. The stage lines grew increasingly restive and demanded a bridge. The ferry had become obsolete.[283]

John Shaw, formerly of the Connecticut Mining Company and now Amos Catlin's partner with the Natoma Mining and Water Company, began construction of a bridge in late 1851. "It was a wooden structure of the common American truss system."[284] Even before it became operational

The drought of 1977 exposed the Mormon Island–Negro Hill Road as it approached the site of the old bridge. Negro Hill is across the water. *CSP.*

In the opposite direction, dike 7 is in the deep background. Schone's saloon was on the right. The school and original Methodist church was nearby. *CSP.*

Left: This 1953 aerial photograph features Mormon Island just east of the bridge, with Negro Hill on the opposite side above. Green Valley Road (Coloma Road) is at the bottom. *UCSB.*

Below: "A Rough Drawing of the Diggins" by Hiram Dwight Pierce features the original church in 1849. It was near the Shaw bridge. *CSP.*

in May 1852, the bridge was damaged by March floodwaters in which a portion was swept away.[285]

After repairs, Shaw applied for a license with the El Dorado Court on April 15, 1852, which entertained jurisdiction on the Negro Hill side of the span. Dallas Kneass made a last-ditch effort to stop the bridge and preserve his ferry service. His appeal was dismissed. After the new bridge survived the winter floods of 1852, the Mormon Island ferry was put out of business.

Top: Jake Hoxsie with his best friend, mid-1890s. This wire suspension bridge was constructed just after the flood of 1862. *CSP.*

Bottom: Residents successfully petitioned Sacramento County for a new bridge. It is seen here during construction in 1908 looking downstream, with Mormon Island on the left. *CSP.*

Shaw's bridge also imposed a toll. The cost for passage ranged from ten cents per person to a dollar for a fully loaded wagon.[286]

In 1854, Sacramento County declared the road from Negro Bar to Mormon Island a public highway. That May, John Shaw petitioned the court to include his quarter-mile spur from the new public highway to the bridge. Shaw's spur was specified by the county to be forty feet wide and stretched south of the "church at the bridge." By having the spur declared a public highway, Shaw no longer had responsibility for its maintenance.[287] Over the ensuing century, Mormon Island and Negro Hill would see the construction of five different bridges. The final and most durable version was built in 1909 and lasted until it was scrapped in 1954, with Folsom Dam on the horizon.[288]

CATASTROPHE AT MORMON ISLAND

On June 23, 1856, a fire broke out in Mormon Island. All of the accounts agreed that the inferno originated in the recently closed Fancy Bakery building, one door west of the Miners Hotel. The fire started at about 1:30 p.m. and, fueled by a canvas roof, quickly spread to the adjoining businesses on the north side of the plaza. Harriet Poor, whose husband, Elijah, was one of Catlin's partners in the Natoma Company, managed the Miners Hotel at the time of the blaze. She barely escaped the disaster, being notified "in so short a time that Mrs. Poor was unable to save her clothing."[289] Ultimately, ten buildings were destroyed, all on the northern side of the central district, which included Darius King's Iron Side business on the northwest corner. Total losses amounted to a shade under $15,000.[290]

Along with the Miners Hotel, King's barbershop and bookstore was a total loss. The smaller Union Hotel, the Bowling Saloon and the Sons of Temperance buildings were also consumed, along with the buildings that housed the shoemaker and the dentistry practice of Dr. Bates. The building that housed the Wells Fargo and the Alta Telegraph companies as well as the post office was also obliterated, but the mail and important papers were salvaged.[291]

Heroic citizens intervened to contain the damage: "Due to the prompt exertion of the citizens and the miners from the immediate vicinity the flames were prevented from crossing the plaza."[292]

The press immediately pointed fingers. Negro Hill, Mormon Island's maligned neighbor, was an obvious target. The *Alta California* of San

Francisco offered this provocative accusation that reeked with bias and provided no direct evidence: "From the fact it was on Saturday as well as because the old bakery was unoccupied, it is presumed the fire was the work of an incendiary. In this we are strengthened by the fact that, on Saturday afternoon, a small building at Negro Hill, on the opposite side of the river was also fired, and it is a notorious fact that the neighborhood is infatuated by a gang of dangerous and suspicious characters."[293]

Three days after the *Alta California*'s publication, the *Placer Herald* offered a more matter-of-fact assessment: "The fire is supposed to have originated from accident."[294]

Fires in nineteenth-century California were as common as a sunny July day. Sacramento City was largely destroyed by fire in 1852. Folsom was devastated by an inferno in 1871. Placerville was almost completely wiped out by a blaze on July 6, 1856, just a mere two weeks after the Mormon Island disaster.[295] While arsonists, or incendiaries as they were known then, caused their fair share of incidents, the accusation itself was commonly used as a cudgel against disfavored races and ethnicities. Australians were a curious target for spurious accusations in the early days of Sacramento,

The Stephenson/Mansion House contained a general store, a post office and a court. Thomas Stephenson was postmaster and justice of the peace for more than twenty years. *CSP.*

Photographed in 1922, the Hoxsie House was the original Mormon Island home of John Bennett, vice-president of the Natoma Company. *CSP.*

but African Americans were also a traditional recipient of suspicion. Negro Hill fit the bill.

The fire at Mormon Island punctuated an already steady decline with the center of gravity shifting southward. The completion of the Sacramento Valley Railroad in 1856, which connected Sacramento with Negro Bar, served as an initial blow. When El Dorado County moved its seat of government from Coloma to Placerville in the following year of 1857, traffic shifted away from the Coloma Road.

The era of individual prospecting dwindled away in favor of more intensive methods such as hydraulic mining. Miners morphed into laborers, and after 1860, Mormon Island entered a pastoral age. The township, which was home to 2,500 residents from 1853 to 1855, rapidly depopulated. By the late 1860s, "traffic to the mines had all but ceased."[296] According to the 1880 census, Mormon Island featured a population of 20, with a regional count of 267, consisting mostly of ranchers and their families along with a few farmhands.[297]

The Exchange Hotel, which escaped the 1856 fire, converted to a general store in its later years. Despite the best efforts of the Native Sons and Daughters, the Exchange was torn down in 1913. Albert Hart, who helped

The old town plaza started at the ravine and extended down the road. The gate on the right led to the original school. *CSP.*

raze the building, commented on its magnificence: "It was remarkably well-preserved, much of the lumber being perfectly sound notwithstanding the many years it has been standing. The manner of construction indicated that in the early days the builders were careful to do substantial work."[298] Plimpton lamented, "Of all the landmarks in Mormon Island, this was the building worthy of preservation."[299] Such a venerable building could have been relocated to Folsom.

RED BANK AND A NEW ERA OF VINEYARDS

By 1853, the Natoma Mining and Water Company, in support of a dam upstream of Salmon Falls, had constructed a maze of ditches and canals that transported water to nearby locations. Larger communities such as Salmon Falls, Negro Hill, Prairie City and Mormon Island took a lion's share, but smaller communities and camps such as Condemned Bar, Massachusetts

Flat and Red Bank enjoyed an ample supply. As surface mining waned in the late 1850s, these waterways increasingly served agricultural interests.

Gold may have originally brought in the first pioneers, but it was agriculture, in particular viticulture, that kept them there. Aside from the water of the "Natoma Ditch," as locals referred to the spider web of canals, two other factors incentivized winemaking and agriculture more broadly. The completion of the Sacramento Valley Railroad (SVRR) in 1856 ensured that agricultural products could be shipped to the eastern United States and beyond. In addition, as prospectors abandoned their claims, land became relatively cheap. As late as 1866, the editors of the *Folsom Telegraph* were imploring local agronomists to increase their real estate holdings or for new farmers to purchase parcels of land from the government and the railroad companies. They argued that it was essential to do this before the completion of the Transcontinental Railroad. The *Folsom Telegraph* punctuated its plea with this exclamation: "The foothills of California will be the great wine district of the state."[300]

From 1880 until the Prohibition era of the 1920s, the region surrounding Mormon Island was a vast expanse of vineyards. Large stone wineries and rolling hills carpeted with vines provided an ambience of a "traditional wine country."[301]

Contemporaries further exclaimed, "The first display of beautiful growing vineyards, covering many hundreds of acres of ground in close connection, and that will stand in comparison with any part of the State may be found now down in the county near Mormon Island."[302]

The virtual entirety of this once immense wine region is now submerged underneath Folsom Lake. Only in low water years, most notably at Red Bank, do cellars and other remnants of a bygone era of viticulture reemerge.

It is best to view Red Bank as "suburban Mormon Island." Located less than a mile east of the main plaza, the locale was, in its origins, a small mining community consisting mostly of Chinese immigrants. Prospectors quickly gleaned the gold from the river side and abandoned the site. Many of these original Chinese American miners would later work the vineyards of the Natoma and Red Bank Wineries.[303]

Henry Mette and his wife, Jennie, left their hometown of Hanover, England, and arrived in Mormon Island in 1851. After a few years of prospecting, the Mettes acquired the Red Bank property and established a winery. By the 1870s, Mette had acquired 375 acres of land, 100 of which were covered in vines. A large cellar was added to the portfolio in 1873. Adjacent to the operation, the couple built a large two-story granite

The Hawk House, a hotel constructed in the 1850s and photographed in the 1880s, was located near the bridge. It was demolished in the 1920s. *CSP.*

mansion, surrounded by an elevated garden that included fig and mulberry trees. A 2-acre olive orchard rounded out the landscape.[304]

The Red Bank winery outlasted Bugbey's Natoma operation, surviving until Prohibition. This was partly due to Henry Mette's connections back east, most notably his brother, who owned a large liquor distributorship in St. Louis. During its peak years, Red Bank produced forty thousand gallons of wine and seven thousand gallons of brandy annually.[305]

The winery featured Zinfandel and Petite Bouchet, among other offerings, but its most successful product was its brandy, which was derived from the Folle Blanche varietal. The 1887 vintage was entered in the Missouri State Fair in St. Louis, capturing "first premium" at the competition.[306] Although the assertion requires further research, it is quite plausible that the Red Bank winery had at least one entry in the 1904 World's Fair.

Tourists frequented tasting rooms in the late nineteenth century much as wine country visitors do today. The Natoma Winery, however, revolutionized hospitality. Bugbey's sparkling wine, which one critic described as sweeter and richer than typical yet nonetheless excellent, inspired a Sacramento musician

The Red Bank winery storage facility was repurposed after Prohibition by the Davies family dairy. *FHM.*

to compose a "Champagne Waltz" and a more up-tempo "Champagne Galop." On one occasion, a candlelight dance attended by twenty guests featured a band whose set list included the "Waltz" and the "Galop." The soiree was held inside a fifty-thousand-gallon wine vat.[307]

Even regular tastings offered the customer unusual flair. One patron marveled, "We found Mr. Bugbey to be one of the most generous, jolly warm men we ever met in any part of the country."[308]

Apparently, sobriety was in short supply. "I believe, in fact, it is boasted that no one ever left the grounds after a second visit-sober," a journalist once reported. "It is rumored that the ex-sheriff regards it as a personal slight to his gold medal brands if the said guests display a sufficient control of 'mind over matter' to be able to reach their vehicles without assistance after taking leave."[309]

Another local winery adjacent to Mormon Island was founded by Hugo and Powell Hart, brothers from Rotterdam in the Netherlands. In addition to their twelve-acre parcel in Salmon Falls, they secured a ranch on the eastern edge of Mormon Island that included an orchard as well as eight acres of vines. By 1879, the Hart winery was producing five thousand gallons.[310]

After Prohibition, the Red Bank winery was purchased by the Davies family, who promptly converted it to a dairy. The Red Bank dairy would remain in operation until the dam began construction in 1954. Jim Davies recalled that after Prohibition, the Hart property was "now planted to pears."[311] The orchard was owned by a Japanese American family until the onset of World War II. After the family was interned at a location unknown, the property fell into foreclosure. "Dr. Johnson," as Davies recalled, purchased the land and maintained the orchard until 1951, upon which, in anticipation of Folsom Dam, the federal government acquired the parcel through eminent domain.[312]

Recalling Jim Davies provides a fitting though tragic end to the Mormon Island story, a saga bookended by the exodus of Mormon families in 1848 and 1849 and the forced exile of a Japanese American family in 1942. The community that was once Mormon Island, the most prestigious of the early California Gold Rush, now resides under a lake.

CHAPTER 7

NEGRO HILL

By Eric Webb and Andrew McLeod

Negro Hill was once home to an interracial community built on a lucrative gold strike. Now submerged behind Folsom Dam, this town has been largely forgotten and even dismissed as a myth. However, one violent incident created a news sensation, breaking the silence that has usually obscured the experiences of African Americans in early California. An examination of documents, including newspaper reports from the gold rush itself, shows this community to have been very real and presents a new glimpse of a period that appears in most imaginations as predominantly white.

The historiography of Erwin Gudde's *Place Names of California*, first published in 1947, is problematic, starting with the fact that he has a single entry for everything starting with "Negro; N…r." He claims that such names were common, "not because there were large numbers of African Americans, but because the presence of a single one was sufficiently conspicuous to suggest calling a place Negro Bar or N…r Slide."[313] The assertion is unsupported, and Gudde does not explain why such a name would repeatedly stick based on a single miner, let alone one not responsible for the discovery.

In contrast, Rudolph Lapp's 1977 *Blacks in Gold Rush California*, a Pulitzer Prize finalist,[314] reveals a gold rush full of African Americans, who mined and lived in significant numbers at numerous locations. Lapp observes that names like Negro Hill "represent sites where a black man made a lucky strike or where groups of black men lived and mined." He notes that by

1852, California was home to more than two thousand African Americans, most of whom lived in the Gold Country, and notes extensive influence from New England abolitionists.

The 1948 California Historical Society annual meeting featured a guest speaker named Reverend John W. Winkley, who recalled his decades of personal experience traveling and preaching throughout the California Gold Country. His meander through dozens of mining camps was briefly summarized in the society's journal. Winkley's findings were listed without critique, except for one prominent rebuttal inserted near the beginning of his talk:

> *In the American River country, the speaker has carefully explored the ruins of such towns as Mormon Island; Prairie City on Alder's Creek, whose only relics are wooden grave makers; Little Negro Hill, the site of which seems an incongruity to us and its story a hoax.*[315]

So, what *was* the story of Negro Hill shared by Winkley, which the society felt necessary to declare a hoax? The present research did not uncover the speaker's notes—if they ever existed—so we cannot discern exactly what claim was being purportedly debunked. However, an examination of newspapers and correspondence from the 1850s reveals a mixed-race community that persisted for years at one of the earliest and richest placer gold strikes. Winkley was onto something.

The New Town

Indeed, the story of Negro Hill is not a hoax; contemporary news accounts confirm that it was a bona fide mining town, located just across the South Fork of the American River from Mormon Island. A ferry connected the two towns in 1849, followed by the Shaw bridge in 1851. Negro Hill resided a few hundred yards upstream from the confluence of the two forks of the American River in the westernmost section of El Dorado County. Evidence suggests that the first prospectors in the vicinity of Negro Hill were the Mormons of 1848, followed by a company of Spaniards, who established a colony known as Spanish Ravine at the tip of the confluence just downstream.[316]

In the fall of 1849, August Newhall, a Methodist minister from Lynn, Massachusetts, and an African American man named Kelsey, who was most

Mormon Island is seen in the foreground; Negro Hill across the river on the shoreline and bluff opposite is connected by the Shaw bridge, circa 1854–55. *SCP.*

likely a minister himself, along with a number of other Bay State African Americans, settled the site later known as Negro Hill. The initial strike in 1849 occurred on the flat along the south fork of the American River.[317] A village quickly sprang up directly across from Mormon Island that became known as Lower, or Little, Negro Hill. The Civil Usage House, a hotel and a general store promptly centered the townscape.[318]

Negro Hill appears fleetingly in the memoir *Fugitive Slave in the Gold Rush: Life and Adventures of James Williams.* The author employs an inconsistent style, varying from detailed word-by-word accounts of entire conversations to broad summaries that give only faint outlines of his travels. Unfortunately, Negro Hill receives the latter treatment. Williams claims to have spent six months in "Negro Hills" but says almost nothing about his time there, even though he went straight to Negro Hill upon arrival in California by sea, spending only a few days traveling from San Francisco. Williams gives no hint how or when he learned of Negro Hill, only saying that it was the "first place I came to." It is curious that Williams did not find this place interesting enough to describe; a fugitive slave and Underground Railroad worker would presumably find half a year in an African American mining town worthy of description. Even stranger, he complains that he "made nothing but my board" during the boom times of May 1851, yet when he left he was leading an equipped group, as evidenced by this statement: "I packed my rocker that we washed the gold with, my prospect-pan and my pick and shovel, and led the way."[319] Williams is not telling us everything, and there is clearly a gap in his narrative.

Nevertheless, reports of successful mining operations buttressed Negro Hill's stature. Early in 1852, the *Union* reported that "rich diggings have been recently discovered, which continue to pay handsomely."[320] The *Alta* soon added that "two sailors took out the handsome sum of [$3,500] above all expenses."[321] In the spring of 1852, on the bluff above Little Negro Hill, Conrad Benninger, Harvey Smith and Darius Clark found "good dirt" on a large flat.[322]

On New Year's Day 1854, the *Empire Argus* of Coloma effused, "This old gold mining locality directly opposite Mormon Island is improving rapidly. A gentleman informs us that about 200 miners are at work and are making fair wages." The report summed up the situation: "Since the introduction of water, business has been quite brisk, money is plenty and the town greatly improved."[323]

Two African American entrepreneurs, also from Massachusetts, opened a boardinghouse and general store, "around which quite a negro village sprung up and was called Big Negro Hill."[324] A bustling, predominantly Black church opened its doors, the faithful shepherded by abolitionist preachers.[325]

White businessmen opened a boardinghouse and a general store on the other side of town. Early California elites joined the venture, such as DeWitt Stanford (the brother of future governor Leland Stanford), who opened a grocery store in 1852. Horace and Frank Barton opened a competing grocery that same year. Benjamin Parke Avery opened a drugstore.[326]

The plentiful and persistent gold of Negro Hill was a powerful attractant, and transportation notices indicate that regular stagecoach lines served the town for at least the mid-1850s. The Shaw ferry, later replaced by the Shaw bridge in 1852, connected the community to Mormon Island and, by extension, the Coloma Road.[327] As a result, Negro Hill became a critical transportation and supply center for the mining towns of the peninsula and upper American River. In November 1854, the Rablin & Company Express Stage began advertising a regular run, thrice weekly, from Sacramento to Negro Hill—"the direct route for the Principal Bars on the American River."[328] By early 1856, a daily stage line was running from Folsom.[329] In 1857, the Alta Express Company introduced a daily express from Chico.[330]

In late 1852, Chinese Americans migrated to the area. While some took residence in Little Negro Hill, even more found a home on the bluff above in Negro Hill. A bustling Chinatown emerged on the "main road, the El Dorado Turnpike, not far from the latter-day school house."[331] By the end of 1853, Negro Hill had developed into a large multicultural community of 1,200 residents, consisting mainly of African Americans, Chinese Americans and European Americans, particularly those of Portuguese heritage.[332] The township was replete "with stores of every description, saloons and dance houses by the dozen, and all seemed to be doing a thriving business."[333]

Newton Miller

Newton Miller, a member of an abolitionist New England family, was born in Vermont in 1827. After a brief stop at Mississippi Bar, he settled in Negro Hill, residing there from 1853 until 1855. Miller's initial residence in Mississippi Bar, albeit for a fleeting few months in late 1852, may have inflamed the inner prejudices that he carried from childhood. Mississippi Bar voted unanimously for proslavery James Buchanan in 1856 and generally had a local culture antithetical to that of the abolitionist stronghold of Massachusetts Flat, located just up the peninsula. Mississippi Bar residents included enslaved African Americans such as Rich and Lucy Brown, whom we'll meet momentarily. Racial relations in the vicinity must have been fraught.

Ultimately, Miller took permanent residence in North San Juan, Nevada County, where he established the Middle Yuba Canal Company. He was a bibliophile and founded the first library in North San Juan. He also started the San Juan Ridge Telephone Company, hailed as the "world's first long distance telephone line." The connection, which was put in service on November 30, 1878, traversed sixty miles with twenty-two stations, "less than three years after Bell spoke from one room to another, two years ahead of Bell's first long distance line, Boston to Providence, 45 miles."[334] In extensive correspondence with his sister, Elizabeth, later discovered in the phone company office, Miller wrestles with his inner demons as he rationalizes his bias.

The letters between Newton and Elizabeth, or Lizzie as he addressed her, also offer an interesting glimpse into life during the heyday of Negro Hill. In an epistle from October 8, 1853, Miller observed that Negro Hill was a dry digging, perched above the water as its name suggests. So fully tapping the hill's wealth would require construction of a canal. The first sign of such an effort can be found in 1853, when a convention of ditch companies met in Sacramento—the Salmon Falls and Negro Hill Canal Company, which was represented by Orlando Jennings and reportedly capitalized at $25,000.[335]

Miller describes, in his correspondence, a comprehensive operational plan for the new Negro Hill tunnel already under construction.[336]

In a subsequent communication from January 8, 1854, Miller details the progress of the tunnel, which was part of a 650-foot canal bored through a bluff along the south fork of the American River.[337] Although this project was one of the smallest valuations listed among conventioneers—perhaps better described as "devalued"—Black, white and Chinese American laborers completed the engineering marvel on schedule in May 1854.[338]

The success of this project inspired others. By 1856, a proposed ditch on the Yuba River pinned its hopes on the investments of "Messrs. Jennings and Fraser, who had been highly successful in a similar enterprise at Negro Hill."[339] In later years, Miller's account of this project enabled the geology and mining departments at the University of California "to set the date of first tunneling nearly two years ahead of previous records."[340] Consequently, the Negro Hill tunnel is now considered to be the first of its kind in the California gold fields.[341]

Newton Miller's letter to his sister on March 13, 1854, would fascinate any psychologist. In it, he discusses his battle with addiction, describing his successful fourteen-month abstinence from tobacco. Fearing a relapse, he offloaded his paraphernalia, which included a pipe, a cigar holder and a candle.[342]

He then describes his battle with bias against African Americans. Miller recounts a childhood story in which a Black neighbor back in New England, a woman named Bess, reacted angrily to the taunts of Miller's classmates. Her understandable response notwithstanding, and even though these children "were perhaps amongst the worst," as Miller admitted, the incident reinforced his prejudice.[343]

Sensing the disapproval of his sister, Lizzie, a newly minted seminarian at Mount Holyoke College who later came to California as an educator, Miller assures her that "any ideas that I may entertain will not cause me to otherwise treat them properly." Perhaps summoning his experience at Mississippi Bar, he ominously notes that "prejudices are much greater here" than in New England.[344]

In his Christmas letter from December 26, 1854, he admits that "charity tells me this prejudice is wrong." Even his minister counsels him as such, but his views were "ingrained" from his childhood.[345] Newton Miller may have kicked his tobacco habit, but he was hopelessly addicted to racism.

He then discusses spiritual life at Negro Hill. Itinerant clergy traveled through the area, such as Father Ingersoll in 1851. However, most were what

Miller described as being from "evangelical denominations."[346] The resident Methodist minister, most likely Reverend Baucher, shared an interesting statistic with Miller; as of May 1852, there had been 26 "evangelical" ministers in California, but by 1854 there were more than 150 serving at least 12,000 congregants.[347]

As for Negro Hill, the prayerful enjoyed ample accommodations:

> *The Methodists have a pretty church—a wooden building with a shingle roof—that will comfortably seat about one hundred persons. There are services in the evening as the minister, who lives in Mormon Island, preaches there in the morning and at Prairie City in the afternoon.*[348]

According to Miller, "nearly all" of the congregants were African American.[349]

Rich and Lucy Brown

State and federal law promoted racial violence in California. A review of the 1850 census for Mississippi Township, which at the time included the area from Mississippi Bar to a point north of Mormon Island, indicates the presence of enslaved people in the region. This included the circumstance of James Brown Sr. and his son James Brown Jr., a father-and-son duo that hailed from North Carolina. They brought with them to California two enslaved African Americans: Rich Brown, twenty-three, also of North Carolina, and Lucy Brown, sixteen, who was born in Virginia. Rich Brown was listed as a cook, while no occupation was signified for Lucy. They were enumerated at a location "above the city (Mormon Island) on the rim," which was the approximate location of Negro Hill.[350]

Three years later, in 1853, James Brown Jr., acting on behalf of his father, secured a writ of arrest from the court of D.H. Taft in Sacramento. Citing the California Fugitive Slave Law of 1852, which mirrored the federal version enacted in 1850, the young couple, Rich and Lucy, were declared fugitive slaves. Although Sacramento County court documents insisted that they "be returned to the Browns immediately" they had, at least for a time, made a successful escape. It remains unclear if they were ever found.[351]

Andrew Jackson and James Taylor

Extrajudicial punishment was common in early California, and African Americans experienced starkly different outcomes compared to their white counterparts. On one occasion in 1853, a young white prospector was caught stealing blankets. After a crowd chased him down, he was subsequently flogged until bloodied. Yet afterward, the crowd "took up a subscription in money and gave it to him with the advice never to steal again."[352]

Not long before this incident, an African American man by the name of Andrew Jackson purportedly stole a "$10 specimen" and some clothes from a Negro Hill blacksmith named Mr. Keith. He was executed by a mob before noon.[353]

A particularly tragic event occurred on January 26, 1853. Charles Nichols, the Mormon Island agent for the Adams Company, wrote an account for the *Sacramento Union* concerning the execution of an African American man named James Taylor. Taylor allegedly stole a gold nugget and some clothing from a couple of Negro Hill residents. The accusation, strikingly similar to the charge levied against Jackson, had the same outcome. Nichols went on to report that a "jury" of twelve white miners "convicted" him in the town square. Immediately thereafter, "The mode of punishment, being left to the mass, it was decided that the prisoner should be executed, they giving him a half hour to arrange his worldly affairs."[354]

Reverend Kelsey, one of the original African American residents of Negro Hill, whom Nichols described as "a very good old man," offered up a final prayer on his behalf. Although some in the mob called for leniency, their voices were drowned out. Taylor was murdered at 4:00 p.m.[355]

Jackson and Taylor were lynched. A court of law would not necessarily have provided justice, however; the California Exclusion Act of 1851 disallowed Black Californians from serving on juries or testifying in a court of law.

Henry Bell

The historical society's claim of a hoax may also be specific, perhaps in reference to a pivotal moment in the life of this community, on March 5, 1855. Two reports appeared in the *Sacramento Daily Union*, both authored by Newton Miller:

A serious stabbing affair occurred at Negro Hill last evening, at the Tracy's House, where a party of blacks and whites were playing at cards. Another party entered the room and commenced the disturbance, whereupon the whites turned against the blacks. A pistol was fired at Henry Bell, (colored), who was afterward mortally stabbed in the left side near the heart. He was a peaceable man, and was stabbed without the slightest provocation.[356]

Monday evening last, there were present in a house or drinking saloon, kept by a negro named Jackson, four whites and three or four negroes, when a gang of rowdies came in drunk and noisy; after some words, one of them seized a bench, which was pulled away from him by one of his own party; in a moment he again seized and threw it at some negroes who were standing behind a table. At the same time, a negro by the name of Henry Bell, was stabbed between the sixth and seventh ribs, by one of the rowdies.[357]

These remarkable accounts, read carefully, reveal a bar run and patronized by African Americans—as well as at least a few white men on at least one occasion. Furthermore, the latter account seems to identify three separate African American parties in addition to the barkeeper. Tracy's was therefore an African American establishment in a town with at least a large minority of African Americans. For such a bar to continue as a going concern, it would need some combination of customers who were either African American themselves or comfortable routinely buying drinks from an African American and consuming them in a thoroughly integrated crowd. The reasons for the presence of the white card players is unclear, and the first account suggests that they may have had hostile inclinations that were brought to the surface by the arrival of their more belligerent peers. On the other hand, the latter account was a rebuttal to the former report.

The fate of Tracy's is unclear; it seems to have operated uneventfully before and after this day, as it apparently made no other appearances in newspapers of the time. But Bell's murder reverberated through the state. Governor John Bigler offered $1,000 for the arrest and conviction of Bell's killers.[358] Then Bigler's Executive Department posted an official proclamation of the reward, which appeared in the *Daily Alta California* on April 5 and was repeated through early August in multiple publications, from the *Shasta Courier* to the *San Joaquin Republican*. It is odd that one of the most powerful people in California would proclaim his support for an obscure murder victim who could neither vote for Bigler nor even testify if he had been a witness rather than a victim of this crime. There is little to indicate why Bigler, whose sympathies aligned with the American South, would have offered a reward for Bell's murder and then advertised it for months. Bell's only other brush with newsworthiness came three years earlier; he was accused of stealing $40 from a barkeeper at the Mechanics' and Traders' Exchange in San Francisco, where he was a steward. He was released after the courts found "not a particle of evidence against" him.[359] Bell was apparently a decent and unremarkable person, who was killed in a setting that reverses the racial expectations of the mythic all-white gold rush—where African Americans appear only fleetingly and lived in a subservient manner due to their lack of right to testify or vote. A Black-owned bar was assaulted by white outsiders, who then became fugitives pursued by the governor of the state of California. It is admittedly a somewhat incongruous tale.

Although the story of Negro Hill—and especially the death of Henry Bell—raises serious questions about race in the gold rush, there does not appear to be any academic work that focuses on this community or this incident. While Shirley Moore's *Sweet Freedom's Plains* tells the story of numerous African Americans on the American frontier—and even examines the family histories of the Gooches and Monroes, who were prominent in nearby Coloma—she does not identify any pioneers who settled or sojourned in Negro Hill.[360] Most sources simply ignore the presence of African Americans, and there is certainly little room for an entire Black community in most mental images of the gold rush.

Justice seemed to be in the offing for Henry Bell. Bigler's announcement had the desired effect, as eyewitnesses identified three suspects by name: Moses Drew, Solomon Rathbun and "Tennessee" or John Murch.[361] At first, "Tennessee" was identified as the main assailant, but later Drew was determined to have been the suspect who actually stabbed Henry Bell.[362]

On April 28, 1855, Trinity County Sheriff William Lowe and his deputy, Marshal Meredith, performed a dramatic arrest of Moses Drew and "Tennessee" in Weaverville. The *Trinity Journal* described the event: "Drew and his comrade came to this place at 11 o'clock on Saturday night." As they were about to leave for Oregon on horseback, "Meredith communicated his suspicions to Lowe, that they were the persons described in the advertisement." They immediately arrested the two men, with Drew admitting that he was the person wanted. "Tennessee," having an obvious propensity for aliases, claimed to be "Newton Dickinson." "Tennessee" had, in his possession, "mining tools and $115 in coin, Drew had a six-inch revolver and a bowie knife but no money."[363]

The adjudication of the Henry Bell case proved anticlimactic. The two suspects were sent to Coloma for trial. In January 1856, both men were set free after being acquitted on all counts, with Drew not only dodging the murder charge but also an additional count of larceny.[364]

Moses Drew should be familiar to local historians. Born in Vermont in 1830, the youngest of eleven children, Drew arrived at Mormon Island in the spring of 1851. After the Henry Bell incident, he briefly worked a claim for Amos Catlin along the Fraser River in 1858.[365]

Drew clearly had an appetite for crime and violence, developing an impressive rap sheet during the 1850s. Before his stint in British Columbia and the murder of Henry Bell, he was arraigned for grand larceny in the El Dorado court in January 1854.[366] He was acquitted the next month.[367] In November 1857, Drew was arrested for assault in Sacramento.[368] After returning from the Fraser River claim, he once again was arrested for assault in Sacramento in January 1859.[369] In each case, charges were either dropped or Drew was acquitted.

Perhaps this should come as no surprise, but after opening a saloon at 6th and K Streets in Sacramento during the early 1870s,[370] Moses Drew was elected sheriff in 1874.[371] He later served on the Board of Equalization starting in 1879 and was appointed to a four-year term as a U.S. marshal in 1881.[372]

In the nineteenth century, allegations of violent crime, particularly against vulnerable communities, were not barriers to leadership in law enforcement. After escaping an attempted murder charge in 1877, with Drew's assistance, Benjamin Bugbey would later succeed his good friend as a U.S. marshal in 1885.[373]

Professor Lapp frames the time of Henry Bell's murder as a high-water mark. He notes growing racism and observes that in the 1856 presidential election, only 22 percent of Negro Hill votes were cast for the antislavery candidate, John Frémont, which Lapp attributes to demographic change. This change was pervasive, however—both Mormon Island and Negro Hill actually voted for Frémont at a slightly higher rate than Mississippi Bar, which voted for Buchanan unanimously, or even its big neighbor downstream, Sacramento.[374]

Nonetheless, African Americans in Negro Hill left for Massachusetts Flat a mile upstream on the north fork side of the peninsula, although the extent of the migration is unknown. In contrast to its neighboring communities and due to its abolitionist origins, 75 percent of residents voted for the antislavery candidate Frémont. Most important, however, according to Lapp, "blacks were never harassed" in Massachusetts Flat.[375]

A NEW ERA

As was the case with Mormon Island and the other mining towns that surrounded Negro Hill, an exodus commenced in the late 1850s as mining entered a more intensive, industrial phase. While the Shaw bridge was "an elegant substantial wire suspension" structure, "the ground around the river had been thoroughly worked over."[376] Ranches, orchards and vineyards overtook the landscape, and by 1860, it was described as a town in retreat. The editor of the *Folsom Telegraph* found "a good grocery store, a saloon, and the scattered cabin homes of miners." Yet there were a number of prospectors in the "neighborhood, most of them Italians and Chinese."[377] The grocery store belonged to Charles Lloyd, who operated it until his death in 1879. By 1885, the last of the original buildings were gone.[378]

Getting to and from Negro Hill was also part of the political calculus of El Dorado County, as revealed during the contentious 1856 decision to relocate the county seat from Coloma to Placerville; the move would significantly increase the distance for many residents of the county. The *Georgetown News* listed seven communities that would be negatively impacted, and Negro Hill was among them.[379] The same list appeared in a follow-up article, which called them "all places of no little importance" and claimed that Negro Hill residents would face an additional twelve miles of travel.[380]

It appears that the first Negro Hill school may have opened as early as 1860 and was situated along the main thoroughfare, the El Dorado

Looking downstream toward the bridge in the 1930s. Mormon Island is on the left and Negro Hill on the right. *CSP.*

turnpike or Negro Hill Road, with some reports marking it close to the Chinatown district. Before the decade ended, however, the school closed, with the few remaining students transferring to the Mormon Island school across the river.[381]

A Baltimore mining company discovered a chrome iron deposit above Negro Hill in the 1880s, with a roster of employees that ranged from eight to twelve.[382] Promising "iron enough in the mountains to supply the whole United States," residents found a need to resurrect the school in order to educate the children of laborers.[383] Although El Dorado school district records list an appropriation for Negro Hill School as early as 1883, multiple accounts place its construction ten years later in 1893.[384]

A few notable families remained, both part of the original Negro Hill elite, who maintained large ranches in the area. Brothers Levi and James Darrington, who emigrated from Bedfordshire, England, came to Negro Hill in 1851. Both men had large families, which populated Negro Hill school with numerous students and the occasional educator. The Darringtons maintained their ranch until the 1950s.[385]

Scotland native Jacob Pilliken, who arrived by way of New York, purchased a large tract of land at Negro Hill in 1858, where he and his family remained until the 1950s. He originally arrived in the region in 1849, prospecting at McDowell Hill and Mormon Island before investing $1,000 in the South Fork Canal Company. After his investment went bad, he replenished his funds upon his return to New York and then remigrated to Negro Hill in 1853. In an interesting twist, he traveled to British Columbia and mined a section on the Fraser River in 1858. It remains unclear whether he accompanied Moses Drew or worked Amos Catlin's claim in Fraser, but it is entirely plausible—both men had run in the same circles for years and most likely knew of each other.[386]

As water from the Natoma Ditch supplied both the Darrington and Pilliken Ranches, California's growing water wars visited Negro Hill in the last decades of the nineteenth century. Three critical episodes highlight the intrigue.

In an affirmation of continued mining interest, the *Placer Herald*, in 1876, reported a new ditch under construction, to take water sixteen miles from near Auburn to Negro Hill, where there were "three or four hundred acres of gravel that they have thoroughly prospected and know to be rich."[387]

A more dramatic event took place in 1883. The California Water Company constructed a canal that connected a new reservoir at Loon Lake with the town of Pilot Hill. In an effort to expand operations, the company expected

Negro Hill school in the 1930s. The school closed in the 1920s and served as an aircraft warning post during World War II. *FHM.*

The Darrington Ranch, as seen in 1954, was located on the northern end of Negro Hill. *CSP.*

This undated photo of the Pilliken Ranch features the original buildings from the 1850s. *CSP.*

water "to be carried in a new ditch from Greenwood Creek over the divide at Pilot Hill to Negro Hill." However, an unknown provocateur sabotaged the effort: "Water from that source never reached the Hill-someone blew up the ditch just below Wild Goose Flat and that company gave up its plan to serve Negro Hill."[388]

Later in 1889, John Hancock, a descendant of original Negro Hill pioneers, bought the Negro Hill Ditch and took over operations. He promptly invested $50,000 in improvements, boring a one-hundred-foot tunnel and in turn repairing and filling in adjacent ditches. Once again, Chinese Americans provided the majority of labor: "Saturday (August 24, 1889) Hancock is working 9 China and 6 White men a half-mile from the dam."[389]

Unfortunately for Hancock, some of the ranchers resented his intrusion, and the Natoma Water and Mining Company, which operated a dam two miles above Salmon Falls, filed a trespassing claim that declared his water rights invalid.[390]

Hancock was no match for a mammoth corporation with deep pockets. A bitter and lengthy legal battle followed that soon took a tragic turn. On February 12, 1892, Hancock's attendant, Walter Noyes, found him hanging inside a miner's cabin in Negro Hill. Although John Hancock's family were convinced that he was murdered, the authorities ruled his death a suicide. At six-foot-three and 240 pounds, they surmised that "it would have taken quite a man to kill him by hanging." The Natoma Company eventually won the lawsuit in 1895, and a diminished water claim passed on to Hancock's grand-nephew George, who resided in Los Angeles.[391]

In a retrospective on Christmas Day 1935, the *Sacramento Bee* reported that there were "two structures on the right of Negro Hill Road (El Dorado Turnpike) hill. A quarter mile farther on was the old Chinese Cemetery, from which all remains had been shipped to China years earlier."[392]

A final commemoration took place in 1953 just before the school was demolished one year later. A crowd of 184 former students, teachers and their families, many of them from the large Darrington clan, assembled at the old school site. They shared reminiscences, telling stories of the reincarnated school and of the old town.[393]

Yet their stories painted an incomplete picture, focusing on the town's second chapter. Negro Hill, especially at its zenith during the 1850s, was not a myth to be swatted away by a racist historical establishment. This was a real and durable Black mining town. Contrary to Gudde's implication that this was merely a place where a "single" Black miner happened to dig, Negro Hill was home to African American as well as Chinese American communities during much of the 1850s. It featured ample gold to drive

The Negro Hill class of 1920. Five of the students and the teacher taking the picture are from the Darrington clan. *CSP.*

economic development and attracted enough people to support regular service from multiple stage lines over several years. Despite California's generally poor and sometimes violent treatment of African Americans and Chinese Americans, Negro Hill had a reasonably stable mixed-race population that was connected to the broader political community of El Dorado County. Negro Hill should therefore provoke historians to reexamine common assumptions about the racial makeup of the people who walked the dusty streets of the Gold Country.

CHAPTER 8

PRAIRIE CITY

By Eric Webb

On November 5, 1950—California's centennial year—a crowd of three hundred people gathered at the presumed site of Prairie City. Surrounded by a vast oak woodland savanna, without a remnant of the old town to be found, citizens traveled from throughout Northern California to pay their respects. A plaque embossed onto granite rock, designated as Department of Natural Resources marker no. 464, was positioned just north of the corner of Prairie City Road and the new federal Highway 50.[394]

Sacramento County Executive Charles Deterding and Supervisor Ancil Hoffman attended the Sunday afternoon affair, but the stars of the show were former residents and their family members. The Native Daughters of the Golden West, in a thoughtful gesture, provided a visitor book, which collected reminiscences of the distant past. "Prairie City is my birthplace," exclaimed Anthony Perry, who drove in from Alameda. Louise Fleming, from nearby Folsom, added, "My folks were married here May 12, 1856 by H.F. Kellum, justice of the peace."[395]

Elizabeth Miller (no relation to Newton) played show-and-tell. She unveiled a locket, made of gold mined at Rhodes Diggings, just a half-mile away. The keepsake was passed down from her great-uncle, Lewis Tomlinson. "He had the locket made in 1850 and presented it to the girl who became his bride in 1854. It contains a daguerreotype of him and on the inside of the cover is engraved 'Lewis to Alta.' Mr. Tomlinson died in 1869. He and his brother

Dr. Len Kidder standing at the site of Prairie City cemetery in 1938. *CSH.*

Abelard are buried in the citizens cemetery there."[396] Little did the attendees know, as was discovered a half-century later, that they stood among Lewis, Abelard and their Prairie City ancestors.

Prairie City, founded in 1853, catapulted immediately into prominence. In the 1856 election, it featured the largest county voting precinct outside the city of Sacramento. By 1860, however, the village was in serious decline and was ultimately degazetted from local maps in 1883.[397] Unlike its neighbors, Mormon Island and Negro Hill, which had residents and structures attesting to its existence, Prairie City's foundations disintegrated into the soil. For many years, not a trace could be found.

Prior to 1853, miners in the region could only employ their techniques in shallow deposits during the rainy season. At first, Kelly's canal routed water from Alder Creek to the mining operations at the future town site.[398] Alexander McKay and his cadre of laborers, many of them Chinese immigrants, built a canal originating in New York Ravine along the south fork of the American River, which begat a web of aqueducts that not only reached Mormon Island but also other mining locales, including Prairie City.[399] In a dramatic turn of events, McKay sold the canal and "all the Dams, Branches, Aqueducts and all the rights, interests, privileges, and advantages to the possession thereof" to the "Natoma Water and Mining Company (NMWC) and to their successors and assigns forever." The parties executed the sale on November 4, 1853, with McKay receiving a relatively small sum of $500.[400]

In another happenstance of history, McKay and the Natoma Company initially planned to terminate their ditch at Rhoads Diggings, which was located about one mile east of Prairie City. They opted, however, to continue the canal another mile to the west in order to connect to Alder Creek. When ditched water reached the area during the summer of 1853, year-round mining was assured and the town was born. The NMWC monopolized water supply ingeniously by recycling water used by local miners, only to charge them once again for the commodity. Not only did the company guarantee delivery during the summer months, but it also assured itself an endless supply of profits.[401]

According to an 1880 account from the *History of Sacramento County* by Thompson and West, Prairie City became an important regional "business town" or supply center that served the nearby mining camps such as "Rhodes Diggings, Willow Hill Diggings and Alder Creek."[402] Water use ledgers of the Natoma Company, as well as the 1857 tax rolls of the Sacramento County Assessor's Office, indicated at least "thirty families [and] a few hundred miners," as well as twenty-seven other individuals in the town.[403] Beyond that, contemporaneous estimates varied but nonetheless accounted for a large population. In April 1854, the *Sacramento (Pictorial) Union* insisted that "the population of Prairie City and vicinity embraces about 2000."[404] Thompson and West simultaneously pegged the population of Prairie City at one thousand.[405]

The term *vicinity*, used by the *Sacramento Union*, may be an important distinction, as it most likely accounted for the surrounding mining camps. This may have included the mysterious village of "Ragtown," located one mile east of Prairie City. Permanent structures, typically made of wood or stone, were a defining characteristic of the mid-nineteenth-century California town. Although scant references to this locale exist, Sacramento County assessor documents from 1857 list a man by the name of J. Southworth who was taxed $20 on personal belongings, as well as $100 on improvements, "indicating that he was probably living in a shelter." More convincingly, Charles Uhlmeyer's residence was simply listed in the county records as being in "Ragtown—one mile east of Prairie City."[406] Otherwise, the fugacious Ragtown never made it to a map; it may have simply "boom and busted" before any cartographer bothered to notice.

Although canvas structures undoubtedly dotted the landscape, Prairie City was more than a "tent city." The lithograph of a woodcut, featured in the New Year's Day 1855 edition of the *Sacramento Daily Union*, shows the substantiality of Prairie City. Aside from the main street with its wagon-cut tracks, two rows of one-story wooden shops can be discerned receding into the background. The woodcut, drawn with "photographic perspective," highlights the store fronts with accuracy. Adams and Company, as well as its competitor, Wells Fargo Express, were common occupants in California mining towns, providing agents "in every considerable mining camp." "M. Beach and Company Clothing," "Queen City" and a generic "Drug Store" bolstered the cityscape. Two doctors set up their respective practices, as well as an additional six shopkeepers.[407]

The *Sacramento Daily Union* noted in June 1853 that two square miles surrounding the "Prairie Surface Diggings," discovered previously in May 1852, had now been claimed in anticipation of the ditch. Forty canvas and wood-frame buildings immediately popped up, with lots going for $100 to $200 each. The next month in July, claims spoked out from the town in a three-mile radius.[408] Within a two-month span, the population ballooned to 1,500, including fifteen families "containing ladies and children." Twenty-by-sixty-foot "corner lots were selling for $500."[409]

Although Dr. Y.A. Massie built the first structure (a hotel), a single carpenter, Elisha Waterman, "erected most of the buildings" in Prairie City. He clearly employed a lot of workers "because, by July 1853, the town is said to have been comprised of 100 buildings, including 15 stores and 10 boarding houses and hotels."[410] Among the enterprises, Jesse Dresser's saloon stood as a favorite watering hole, as well as "the largest general merchandise store," which was opened in 1854 by the brothers John and James Spruance.[411] "Two lines of stages were running daily" connecting the town with Sacramento, as well as its sister mining towns in Mormon Island and Negro Hill. The Rablin and Company Express offered connections from Sacramento, originating from 2nd and K Streets at 7:00 a.m. on Tuesday, Thursday and Saturday, with return trips on Monday, Wednesday and Friday.[412]

In a letter to the *Sacramento Union*, a local miner described the preferable conditions of Prairie City:

> *Miners from the northern region are daily crowding in upon us, and tell us that many more are coming, and that as soon as those who are in the rivers are driven out by the rain, they will come down from the mountains into these regions, where the mines are equally as good—if not better—and provisions much cheaper. They say the immense suffering and hardships they underwent last winter is a dread upon them, and they are determined to seek more comfortable quarters for the approaching season.*[413]

Prairie City, just as in Negro Hill, included a vibrant Chinatown. In the April 1854 edition of the *Sacramento Pictorial Union*, Prairie City became "a favorite resort for Chinese men, large numbers of whom have taken up their residence in the neighborhood and work the refuse portions of the ground with much assiduity."[414]

Yet almost as quickly as Prairie City blossomed, it promptly withered away. The slackening of the town can be closely correlated to the exhaustion of surface gold throughout California. California gold production peaked at just over $81 million in 1852, leveled out at $70 million in 1853 and plummeting to just under $46 million in 1859. The 1860s saw a further decline with receipts totaling $23 million in 1863 and then bottoming out at $17 million in 1866.[415]

Chinese immigrants, already a significant presence in the Prairie City community, increased their majorities in the local labor force as the town disintegrated. In 1854, Natoma Company water ledgers accounted for 176 miners, a somewhat misleading number given that at least 60 of these "miners" were actually mining "companies" in and of themselves. By 1866, the NMWC listed only 48 names, none of which included any other mining companies, another indication of the company's evolving monopoly. Of these 48, 34 "are Asian names, plainly indicating the presence of Chinese in the area after many of the original miners, representing several ethnic groups but mostly of European extraction, had left."[416] An 1869 description of the region maintains "that not more than 500 miners were taking water from the Natoma Ditch to wash placer gold at Red Bank, Mormon Island, Willow springs, Rhodes Diggings, Texas Hill, Alder Creek, Rebel Hill, Tates Flat and Prairie City." All except Red Bank and Mormon Island were within a three-mile radius of Prairie City.[417]

In the 1853 election, 364 voters turned out, with votes cast dropping in the next two years to 235 and 183. A "special" plebiscite on March 28, 1855, resulted in an objection to the formation of the Sacramento County Board of Supervisors. This local election, overseen by Justice of the Peace H.F. Kellum, also appointed Alexander McKay to the school commission, perhaps in consolation for his sale of the New York Ravine canal.[418]

But the decline in voter rolls offered further evidence of Prairie City's diminution. In the presidential election of 1856, 213 cast their ballot at the main hotel, the Marble Hall, with the majority supporting James Buchanan over the first National Republican party candidate, John C. Frémont. Turnout dropped to 115 in 1857, even though "the city" was the "principal place for what was then called Granite Township." In 1860, after two years of dwindling voter participation, 100 citizens stuffed the ballot box, with 15 filled out in favor of Abraham Lincoln.

Seventy-eight voted in the 1863 election and then fifty in 1864. Prairie City was clearly a Democratic town, with only fourteen voters favoring Lincoln over George McClellan. After the 1864 election, the voting precinct disappeared. What once had been the second-largest election center in Sacramento County simply vanished.[419]

Geography contributed to Prairie City's downfall. The town was equidistant from Coloma Road to the north and the Sacramento-Placerville Road to the south. Unlike Mormon Island and Negro Hill, Prairie City was not situated near perpetual water; rather, it was entirely dependent on the Natoma Ditch, with nearby Alder Creek a mere seasonal stream. By 1856, Folsom not only had river and road access but also overtook neighboring towns as the terminus of the Sacramento Valley Railroad.

As placer gold disappeared, people moved on from Prairie City. Frank McNamee, who emigrated from County Cavan, Ireland, resided and mined in Prairie City for three years before moving to Folsom in 1857. Taking advantage of the new railroad, he opened a mercantile store, overseeing it well into the 1880s, whereupon his wife took over. Back in Prairie City, by 1876, "there was nothing but a school building," which was later relocated, and "the ruins of an old livery stable and one cabin, where some miners live."[420] The livery stable was previously owned by John King Luttrell, who,

An automobile crosses Alder Creek at Prairie City in 1938. The cemetery is on the hill at the upper left. *CSH.*

at that very time in the 1870s, represented California in the U.S. House, in yet another testament to Prairie City's prior preeminence.

Intensive gold mining cannibalized the Prairie City townsite. As bucket line dredging and other innovations took hold at the turn of century, the Natoma Company labor force consisted of an increasing percentage of Chinese immigrants. Archaeologists have unearthed numerous sites in the area, discerning locations inhabited by both European Americans and Chinese Americans.

Perhaps the most compelling of these sites is what California Department of Transportation archaeologists refer to as "Locus 29." Currently situated beneath Highway 50 one mile east of the Prairie City interchange, this may have been, at first, the site of Ragtown. Not long after, Locus 29 encompassed living spaces for local laborers. Anthropologists documented a segregated neighborhood along a tributary of Alder Creek: "Of particular interest at this site is the fact that rock hearths and Chinese artifacts were found only on the west side of the drainage. To the east were no Chinese materials or features, only Euro-American artifacts and rectangular, rock-supported features and pads identified."[421]

Chinese American laborers also resided in barracks provided by the Natoma Company, one of which was located in Blue Ravine, near the current intersection with Folsom Boulevard; another stood at Willow Creek nearby. They would then travel to the mining sites on a daily basis.[422]

In the 1940s, a decade prior to the centennial celebrations, workers paving the new U.S. Highway 50 uncovered shards of headstones. But no real effort was made to locate the Prairie City cemetery. The workers merely reburied what they found.[423]

Armed with the 1966 National Historic Preservation Act a half-century later, archaeologists initiated a more concerted effort to locate the cemetery as Caltrans constructed the new Prairie City Road–U.S. 50 interchange. Historians and scientists obtained even more evidence for their dossier. Maps from the 1860s suggested that the proposed interchange laid directly on top of the erstwhile town with its cemetery on "top of a knoll in the northwest quadrant of the interchange." Using remote sensing technology and mechanical equipment, archaeologists exhumed twelve Prairie City residents and promptly transported their remains to the Caltrans pathology laboratory. Of the twelve, anthropologists identified seven adults and five children.[424]

Upon the construction of the freeway interchange in 1997, "thirteen fragments from marble headstones and three granite headstone bases" were

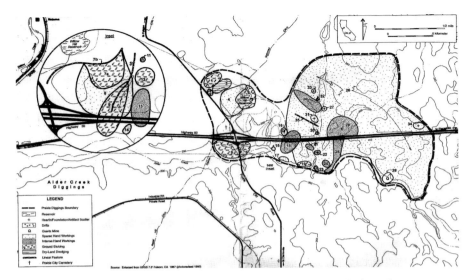

A map of the Prairie City region. Of note is Locus 29. The cross at the interchange indicates the cemetery. *CalTrans.*

found buried underneath the surface, none of which "appeared to be in its original location." One of the granite bases was uprooted by a tree, otherwise the fragments, all from disparate headstones may have been "buried together as a sign of respect." Mabel Brown, whose ranchland encompassed the knoll that housed the cemetery, "found and reburied several headstones from the cemetery" during highway construction in the 1940s.[425]

As archaeologists excavated the cemetery in preparation for the construction of the Prairie City Road interchange, they discerned headstones of similar design. All of the fragments displayed images of flowers, with one piece featuring a representation of a weeping willow, all common Romantic era motifs in nineteenth-century graveyards. Although the headstones were derived from the same type of marble, their edges and thickness varied. Presumably, the markers were manufactured locally, but they differed in design from cemeteries in Folsom and Sacramento, perhaps indicating their origin in the 1850s, when gravestones were somewhat less homogenous. As for the inhabitants of the Prairie City cemetery, a vast majority of their identities remain a mystery. Decades-old headstone fragments offer few clues and cannot be reconstructed to provide any names.[426]

Death notices, however, from local papers and from Trinity Episcopal Church in Folsom deliver better results. Some of those who died at Prairie City included William Gunn, Catherine Gertrude Turner, Warren Morse,

Dr. Kidder standing next to a headstone at the cemetery in 1938. *CSH.*

George Elmond, Julia Theresa Bremond and an infant with the surname McKarnan. Most of these people died between 1853 and 1858, and it is not known whether these residents were reunited with other family members or perhaps buried in Folsom, Sacramento or elsewhere. A small number of townspeople were buried in the cemetery in subsequent decades, with the last interment most likely G.W. Mayberry, "who died at this home, described as Prairie City, in 1898." Many of the deceased were undoubtedly miners, but others may have been involved with the numerous saloons, stores and various enterprises within the city.[427]

Evidence strongly indicates the presence of the O'Hara family at the Prairie City cemetery. Berniece Timberlake, her testimony substantiated by records from Trinity Episcopal Church and local newspapers, was the granddaughter of Margaret Ellen O'Hara, who was born in Prairie City in 1863, the youngest of four children. Margaret Ellen's parents, Michael O'Hara and Mary O'Hara (Donnelly), arrived from Ireland sometime in 1853 to try their luck as gold miners. Aside from Margaret Ellen, the other three O'Hara children were Mary, Annie and James.

The O'Hara descendants became prominent figures in Folsom. Margaret Ellen would later marry another Irishman, Tom Foley, in 1880. After fighting for the Union in the Civil War, he spent his later career as a guard at Folsom Prison. Other extended relatives enjoyed significant positions in local water businesses; Will Rowlands was a dredge master for the Natomas Company, and Charles Goulden worked as a carpenter for the Capital Dredge Company in the early twentieth century.[428]

Tragedy had struck the early O'Hara ancestors in rapid succession. The lone son, James, died at nearby Rhodes Diggings on January 13, 1870. Just a few weeks later, his father, Michael, died at the age of forty-five. His widow, Mary, remarried and left town but was promptly abandoned by her new husband and returned to Prairie City in 1872. She would die shortly thereafter. One of the three daughters, Annie, died at the age of fourteen sometime in the early 1870s. All four members of the O'Hara family are presumed to be interred at the Prairie City cemetery.

George Crooks was another well-known inhabitant during Prairie City's most vibrant timeframe between 1853 and 1855. According to California State Parks historian John Plimpton:

Crooks was originally from Scotland, where his name was spelled "Cruicks." Trained in his home country as a carpenter and cabinet maker, he was 28 when he arrived in Prairie City to try his hand at mining; he worked with two partners. While there, he and his wife had a son, who soon died, and a daughter. Crooks' success as a miner was not spectacular and in 1855 he managed to find work as a carpenter helping to repair the Natoma Company's long flume over New York Ravine, south of Salmon Falls. Crooks secured a position in the Natoma Company as a water agent and foreman in 1857, a job he would maintain until his retirement 43 years later.[429]

Conclusion

In the *Sacramento Union*'s January 7, 1906 edition, the Folsom correspondent composed an elegy for Prairie City:

Prairie City was located a few miles south of Folsom, on the road to Michigan Bar, but if any of the men who dug gold dust about there and who used to sell their dust in the busy town were to return after the lapse of fifty-five years that have intervened, it would puzzle them to point out the spot where Prairie City stood, with its streets, its stores and hotels, for there has not for many long years been a vestige of the place to be seen. Instead of the red-shirted and high-booted miners, the only denizens of the gulch have been cows, jack-rabbits and coyotes. Where merchants at one time did a thriving business, and the rattle of stage wheels were heard all the day through, the solitude is broken now only by the occasional shot from some quail hunter's gun, the tinkle of cowbells, and the doleful nocturnal yelp of the coyote…

Some twenty years ago an old stage driver who still pilots a mud wagon through that locality on its tri-weekly trip to the Cosumnes, used to call the attention of his passengers to a little heap of stones, which he said was once a part of the foundation of a building that at one time was a Prairie City hotel. Now even that little pile of stones has toppled over, and the old stage driver's trips have ceased. He too, has disappeared from the earth as completely as had the Prairie City of other days.[430]

In 1960, Plimpton added an exclamation to the *Union*'s epitaph:

There is nothing left of the town of Prairie City, true, there is a house or two in the area, but they were built long after the town folded. [Prairie City] fell victim to the Gold Dredger shortly after the turn of the century and again in the 1930s, thus nothing is left to mark the sites except pile on pile and row on row of rock tailing, left by those dredgers after the earth was dug to a depth of some 40 feet and the gold lodged in it removed.[431]

As today's traveler encounters the environs surrounding the vanished townsite near the highway interchange, a visage of natural resilience takes shape. The stark, barren landscape of the early twentieth century, pockmarked with placers, is now obscured by oak woodland and grasslands. Endemic vernal pool complexes, though highly fragmented, remain in the area, some of which are protected at Prairie City OHV State Park.

The history of Prairie City provides a cautionary reminder. Modern Folsom development will soon extend south of the old cemetery and highway, its tentacles reaching into the obscured cobble of dredging and aqueducts of a gold field and town satiated only with the diversion of water. Memories of Prairie City fade at our peril.

AFTERMATH

By Andrew McLeod

The *Sacramento Daily Union* of January 21, 1857, included a startling announcement: Lewis Sanders Jr. would auction off vast swaths of land, including four-hundred-foot sections of Sacramento City's waterfront. Sanders sought to resolve "certain debts of Wm. Muldrow and others."[432] Despite the absurdity of this massive blackmail against numerous properties' recognized owners, Sacramento stopped in its tracks, with "no small degree of excitement and indignation" reported in town.[433] The city itself filed suit to stop the sales. The *Union* churned out column inches of analysis countering a claim that should ordinarily have been met with raucous laughter. The auction was eventually postponed after a few tumultuous weeks because "the parties have not yet ascertained what lots they are, in their own estimation, entitled to sell."[434]

Seven years after the Squatters' Riot, Sacramento's title troubles were far from over. And while Sanders's wild bet did not pay off, it laid the groundwork for another decade of turmoil, with Muldrow playing a central role. The following year, the two rogues began work on their bizarre *Map of the Partition of Sacramento City*, which carved most land northwest of the Larco Line into their competing claims.

And Muldrow was just getting started. In April 1868, he inaugurated the Ejectment Suits, a legal battle royale involving most Sacramento real estate. As the *Union* reported, "Everybody seems inclined to bring suit against everybody else."[435] No county map books older than 1870 survive to help untangle the origins and impacts of this renewed turmoil, but it was clearly catastrophic. At one point, the *Union* devoted its front and back cover—usually lucrative ad space—to a dense list of more than seven hundred lawsuits. Among these were seventeen brought by Muldrow, including no. 11,991, against hundreds of "possessors, occupants and owners" of everything between the centerlines of I and L Streets, running the grid's entire length. Muldrow thus claimed ninety blocks of Sacramento's most valuable real estate, as well as the streets themselves.[436] Some of his other sixteen suits were nearly as wild. Sacramento should have shrugged. Instead, it panicked. And no known historian has ever examined the resulting legal free-for-all in which the attempted seizure of the city's main drags was buried in nearly two pages of dense newsprint.

Nor has history reckoned with what came next. Faced with a seemingly permanent state of chaos, some Sacramentans turned to a cooperative solution called homestead associations. The Sacramento City Extension Homestead Association, for example, saw itself as part of the "best and often the only method by which those of small means may be possessed of real estate and the ownership of homes."[437] It bought 265 acres adjacent to Sacramento City and subdivided the land into 900 parcels. Despite bootstraps rhetoric and anti-speculation bylaws, its founding members included Leland Stanford, Mark Hopkins, C.P. Huntington and Charles Crocker—the Big Four of railroad fame—along with Crocker's brother Edwin, whose former home now holds the West's oldest art museum.[438] But despite leadership including some of California's heaviest hitters, this innovative community development tool went nowhere. "Homestead" was still mapped on the R Street tracks in 1893.[439] But the utopia was gone; its land was eventually replatted with a rail-side cannery at its heart. Even this profoundly well-connected attempt to build a protective wall around shared holdings, evidently in hopes of repelling the likes of Sanders and Muldrow, mysteriously came to naught.

This presumably powerful association's demise may be explained by a subtle clue on the 1913 *Map of Sacramento City* by Phinney, Cate & Marshall. At first glance, this map is standard modern cartography, an accurate and detailed reference including the city's latest growth. But a closer look reveals ghosts of a Sacramento that could have been, shown by faint superimposed lines: Norristown and Sutterville float across the land, along with Slater's Addition and El Calle de los Americanos. And just beyond the boundaries of the old Sacramento City grid lies a strange pair of disturbances flanking the Big Four's uncharacteristically communalist effort: Both Folsom Boulevard

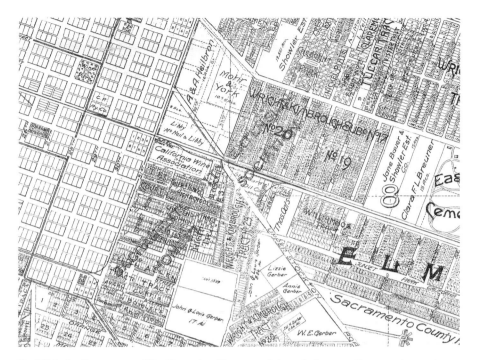

By 1913, the Sacramento City Extension Homestead Association was disappearing under new subdivisions, including the realignments of both Folsom Boulevard and Y Street. *CSH.*

and Y Street were moved outward, separating road access from both sides of their tract and perhaps scuttling the project. The Big Four were usually game for a land fight, but here they seem to have quietly walked away.

RACE TO THE BOTTOMLANDS

Sacramento's turbulent past left a topsy-turvy legacy. The worst land became most valuable. The best land was squandered. Towns that once served as life rafts for flood refugees were reduced to a few shattered boards bobbing in the wake of an "indomitable city," steaming through history. Sacramento City survived against all odds—and against the animal impulse to seek high ground when the water rises. And modern Sacramento has clung to its blissful ignorance of repeated large-scale dispossession, avoiding notice of the municipal debris in the water while sipping drinks topside. Historians have reduced a complicated web of conflicting land claims to "squatter trouble," with legitimacy rooted solely in the unholy alliance between Sutter's claim and Sacramento City's proprietors. Everyone else slipped beneath the waves.

But some have remembered. Phinney, Cate & Marshall's subversive cartography and F.J. Klaus's Norristown forensics may be the only surviving depictions of growth's costs (although more will hopefully emerge). Their century-old wave of interest was perhaps stirred by Sacramento city limits expanding into territory formerly reckoned as streets and parcels of Sutterville and Norristown—a massive 1911 annexation extended Sacramento miles eastward and southward. This more than doubled the city's territory and evidently sated its hunger until 1946, when it nibbled on its former neighbors' remains with a trio of small expansions kicking off the era of postwar suburban sprawl. The American River waterfront—disgorged sometime after 1854—would not be fully reingested until 1960.[440] The city's midcentury expansion spree likely unearthed a few cadastral bodies, whose burial sites lurk in ordinarily mundane deeds and plats, quietly awaiting an attentive eye.

Urban corpses lie in shallow graves along a haunted riverside that remains a vast and surprising blank spot. Ordinarily attractive places are instead curiously repulsive. Setting aside important political questions about public versus private amenities, the latter's absence is especially curious. Downstream of Old Sac and the Miller Park Marina, there's nothing commercial until a hotel and restaurant a few miles downstream—on the far side of Sutterville's vanished waterfront. And ever since the 2008 closure of the Rusty Duck, Sacramento lacks a single place to enjoy dinner or drinks along the gloriously scenic lower American River. Public parkways certainly maintain much of the commercial void. But they fail to explain its origin, which clearly predates modern protective designations.

Hoovervilles of the 1930s were a particularly ironic echo of Sacramento's first squatter episode. The Great Depression, like the gold rush, brought an influx of landless people, unable or unwilling to pay for a place to live. Shantytowns erupted on what seemed like marginal land in the twentieth century. But in the early days, these were *obviously* the best places to live, clustered along the very same levees on which Sacramento City's first map showed preexisting settlement—relatively high and dry. These critical sites are now oddly vacant.

Even today, nearly 175 years after the Squatters' Riot, Sacramento's waterfronts are home, mostly, to squatters. Only people without means to live elsewhere have persistently lived here. They have struggled to build makeshift dwellings along the ancient levee lands, sometimes with rudimentary community organization. Meanwhile, the city pursues policies that destroy their humble homes, leaving flotsam and jetsam swirling in the eddies of urban growth. Although the modern homelessness crisis is nearly universal for American municipalities, Sacramento's version is particularly poignant in the light of the city's long struggle to determine who has the right to live where. Today's unhoused Sacramentans are not much like the squatters of yore, but both stand at points on a progression of diminishing access to land in the West.

When the Sacramento Settlers' Association met to challenge the city's speculators, it often gathered en masse on "the levee." This was most likely the high ground upstream of Sutter's Embarcadero, at the confluence. And according to Eifler, Settler leader Dr. Robinson built a cabin "at the foot of I Street" as the conflict escalated—again, on the levee—which was soon destroyed by Sam Brannan's "informal merchant militia."[441] Robinson eventually gave up on Sacramento and took his talents to Kansas. There he rose to become the state's first governor. What and who else has Sacramento lost in its dogged quest to protect speculators' interests?

Impoverished and improvised communities keep springing up on land that was (and remains) superior to the city core in two essential ways: it is both closer to the river and less likely to be flooded. But Sacramento City's hegemony inverted land values while killing off competing communities. This concentration of wealth and power came at tremendous cost. When it comes to urban flood hazards, Sacramento is second only to New Orleans, a city whose similar topography generated the nation's most tragic modern flooding. While Sacramento's rivers have been kept in check for the last century, climate change increases the chances of a levee break that could rival or dwarf the 2005 catastrophe.

Sacramento didn't have to be this way. Specific intentional land use decisions formed the city, and many of these decisions were evidently made primarily for private short-term gain at great cost to collective safety. Even as flooding became a clear and persistent threat, urban design protected investments in the least defensible place—that predatory land scheme known as Sacramento City. Sunk costs kept adding pressure to this motivation. Each subsequent decision may have made sense, but the string of decisions had disastrous consequences that were already clear by the great flood of 1862.

The worst of Sacramento's flood problems could have been avoided through continued growth from multiple urban centers—from these Lost Sacramentos. Sutter's Embarcadero was just one of several options available

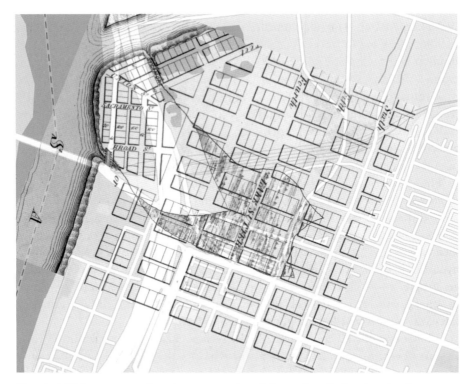

Slater's Addition once stood on the western edge of the modern Railyards redevelopment area, between I-5 and the river (LOC, Esri). *Andrew McLeod.*

to newcomers, and the others could have helped build a more robust metropolis. A successful gold rush city needed a riverbank that was high enough to avoid most flooding in the winter, but it also needed a channel that was deep enough for large vessels to dock—this was especially challenging in the summer and fall, when rivers ran very low. The other main amenity to determine a site's viability was eastward land access to the mines and northerly connection to overland trails that brought in new arrivals. A variety of waterfronts would have yielded a much more resilient city.

Lost Sacramentos had their tradeoffs, of course. But each site's flaws fail to account for their collective disappearance. Flooding was supposedly the problem in Sutterville. However, that town also included some of the highest land near the Sacramento River, as well as a reliably dry route toward the mountains. Title trouble supposedly did in Brighton, but nobody has ever really explained who held the better title. Norristown simply died without explanation. Hoboken was dismissed as an ephemeral gathering that dissipated on its own when the waters subsided from Sacramento City, but the presence of several wood-frame buildings clashes with the history handed down by the Sacramento City establishment—this was no simple camp. Although Negro Hill and Mormon Island declined more typically, it is remarkable that these foundational communities—and the riverside transportation network they anchored—became so expendable and thoroughly forgotten. Prairie City may have lacked water for sustainable growth before canals were constructed, but even the driest diggings left their obvious marks. And besides, canals *were* constructed.

These diverse disappearances must be explained.

Perhaps coercion shut down Lost Sacramentos. Perhaps actual violence backed the apparent intimidation that would best explain entire communities disappearing without historic notice. These are certainly controversial ideas that require much further scrutiny. However, this intentional removal hypothesis best accounts for the wide array of irregularities in the history and geography of Sacramento. Hopefully other researchers will take up some of the questions raised here, and broader participation will help identify relevant sources that have so far escaped notice.

What does this all mean today? These long-past events offer important lessons about what we remember and what we forget—important lessons in today's fraught political environment. Entire communities can entirely escape our memory. This means that the present decade's attempts to install a false history might actually succeed! And Sacramento's past shows us what such a success might look like. Obviously the technology and social contexts are hugely different now, but similar historic purges cannot be ruled out. Indeed, they are underway. If we're not careful, revisionist historians will need to sort out America's current predicament generations from now.

As for geography, we should not be too attached to the shape of Sacramento as we find it today. The design was a bad idea. The modern city has made the best of things, but it's still a dangerous spot to face the rising waters of climate change. Some key sites were held dormant for years before eventual suburban redevelopment made a not-quite-clean slate. Lost Sacramentos are mostly abandoned, except for the growing crowds of unhoused people who echo the "squatters" of yore. Many of these locations are underdeveloped and available for adaptive reuse to face uncertain but increasing flood risks.

We should recall what we lost and recognize what remains. Just north of Old Sac, just beyond the I Street Bridge, stands a derelict brick building.

The Sacramento Gas Works ruins still stand on the former Slater's Addition waterfront, just upstream of the I Street Bridge. *Meghan Vanderford.*

It is flanked by a long string of mostly buried waterfront structures. This was once Slater Addition's 1st Street. This was probably the levee where the Settlers gathered. Now a stretch of waterfront rooflines juts from the earth, eroding into the river. It is a layered ruin with no interpretation, rotting away in the open air. And it is fortified to keep out modern squatters. Even now this place is contested.

NOTES

Introduction

1. Theodore Judah, *Map of the Town of Folsom* (1855), online at https://archive.org/details/map1979080007.
2. USGS, *Brighton Quad* (1911), online at https://ngmdb.usgs.gov/topoview/viewer.
3. Mark Eifler, *Gold Rush Capitalists: Greed and Growth in Sacramento* (Albuquerque: University of New Mexico Press, 2002), 155.

Chapter 1

4. Browsing various cities in Google Maps facilitates discernment of Sacramento's unique scarcity of historic waterfronts; that platform will generally serve as a valuable companion to this book.
5. The Burke Museum's Waterlines Project offers a remarkable depiction of shoreline changes that made Seattle's waterfront possible. View online at www.burkemuseum.org/static/waterlines/project_map.html.
6. Robert Kelley, *Battling the Inland Sea* (Berkeley: University of California Press, 1989), 5.
7. "Mass Meeting and Election," *Placer Times*, May 5, 1849.
8. Damon B. Akins and William J. Bauer Jr., *We Are the Land: A History of Native California* (Berkeley: University of California Press, 2021), 121.
9. L.W. Sloat, *Map of Sacramento City*, in *1853–54 Sacramento Directory*, ed. Mead Kibbey (Sacramento: California State Library Foundation, 1997).

10. Cadwalader Ringgold, *Chart of the Sacramento River* (1852), Stanford University, online at www.davidrumsey.com/maps890049-24358.html.

11. E. Gould Buffum, *Six Months in the Gold Mines* (Philadelphia, PA: Lea and Blanchard, 1850), 153–54.

12. "The City of Boston," *Sacramento Record Union*, June 18, 1886.

13. Eifler, *Gold Rush Capitalists*, 146–47.

14. Eifler, *Gold Rush Capitalists*, 135.

15. *The Sutter Alvarado Grant* (1850), Bancroft Library, online at https://calisphere. org/item/ark:/13030/hb8870094b.

16. Mary Floyd Williams, ed., *Papers of the San Francisco Committee of Vigilance of 1851* (Berkeley: University of California Press, 1919).

17. Nancy J. Taniguchi, *Dirty Deeds* (Norman: University of Oklahoma Press, 2016), 5.

18. Eifler, *Gold Rush Capitalists*, 189–90.

19. "Prospectus," *Settlers' and Miners' Tribune*, October 30, 1850.

20. Hubert Howe Bancroft, *History of California*, vol. 6 (San Francisco, CA: History Company, 1888), 329–35.

21. Eifler, *Gold Rush Capitalists*, 188.

22. "Immense Excitement!" *Sacramento Transcript*, February 26, 1851.

23. John F. Morse, *History of Sacramento*, in *1853–54 Sacramento Directory*, ed. Mead Kibbey (Sacramento: California State Library Foundation, 1997), 69.

24. Library of Congress, Chronicling America, online at www.chroniclingamerica. loc.gov.

25. "The Long Agony," *Steamer Index*, February 26, 1851.

26. Marianne Leach, *Newspaper Holdings of the California State Library* (Sacramento: California State Library, 1986), 300.

27. "City Intelligence," *Daily Alta California*, June 8, 1851.

28. "The Execution of Jenkins," *Daily Alta California*, June 12, 1851.

29. "Sacramento," *Daily Alta California*, June 28, 1851.

30. "A Dastardly Attack," *Transcript*, April 14, 1850.

31. Thomas H. Thompson and Albert Augustus West, *History of Sacramento County, California*, 1880 (reprint, Berkeley, CA: Howell-North, 1960), 125–26.

32. Morse, *History of Sacramento*, 70.

Chapter 2

33. Heinrich Lienhard, *A Pioneer at Sutter's Fort, 1846–1850*, ed. Marguerite Eyer Wilbur (Los Angeles, CA: Calafia Society, 1941), 87.

34. Johann Sutter to Pearson Reading, January 29, 1846, Box 285, Pearson B. Reading Collection, California State Library, Sacramento, CA.

35. Johann A. Sutter, *New Helvetia Diary* (San Francisco, CA: Grabhorn Press, 1939), 26.

36. James P. Zollinger, *Sutter: The Man and His Empire* (New York: Oxford University Press, 1939), 190.

37. Johann Sutter to William Hartwell, December 13, 1844, Box 312, John Augustus Sutter Collection, California State Library, Sacramento, CA.

38. Johann Sutter to Pearson Reading, February 8, 1846, Box 285, Pearson B. Reading Collection, California State Library, Sacramento, CA.

39. Eifler, *Gold Rush Capitalists*, 36.

40. Brain McGinty, "Could One of These Have Been the City?'" *California History* (Spring 1985): 133.

41. Daniel Pisani, "Squatter Law in California, 1850–1858," *Western Historical Quarterly* (Autumn 1994): 278.

42. Johann Sutter to Unknown, May 4, 1845, Box 312, John Augustus Sutter Collection, California State Library, Sacramento, CA.

43. Johann Sutter to Unknown, May 18, 1845, Box 312, John Augustus Sutter Collection, California State Library, Sacramento, CA.

44. Walter W. Weir, *Soils of Sacramento County California* (Berkeley: University of California Press, 1950), 46.

45. "Notice," *Daily Placer Times and Transcript* (Sacramento, CA), February 2, 1850.

46. Theodore Van Dyke, T.T. Leberthon and A. Taylor, *City and County of San Diego* (San Diego, CA: Leberthon and Taylor, 1888), 158.

47. Van Dyke, Leberthon and Taylor, *City and County of San Diego*, 158.

48. Carl Abbott, *Portland in Three Centuries: The Place and the People* (Corvallis: Oregon State University Press, 2022), 24.

49. Johann Sutter to Victor Prudon, May 18, 1845, and January 1, 1846, Box 312, John Augustus Sutter Collection, California State Library, Sacramento, CA.

50. Bruno Schmolder, *Neuer Praktischer Wegweiser fur Auswanderer nach Nord-Amerika: In Drei Abtheilungen mit Karten, Planen und Ansichten* (Mainz: Le Roux'sche Hofbuchlandlung, 1849), 79. Schmolder visited Sutter's Fort in 1847 and eventually wrote a travel guide for the American West. Fond of Sutter and certainly interested in city building, Schmolder included a projected map of Sutterville in the guide.

51. Lyle F. Perusse, "The Gothic Revival in California, 1850–1890," *Journal of the Society of Architectural History* (October 1955): 15.

52. "Old Letter Relates Vicissitudes of Argonauts: Impressions Perpetuated by Arrival of 1849," *Oakland (CA) Tribune*, May 23, 1926.

53. Johann Sutter to Pearson Reading, January 29, 1846, Box 312, John Augustus Sutter Collection, California State Library, Sacramento, CA.

54. "New Helvetia," *The Californian*, July 15, 1848; Johann Sutter to H.W. Halleck, June 25, 1847, Box 312, John Augustus Sutter Collection, California State Library, Sacramento, CA; Johann Sutter to Thomas O. Larkin, December 20, 1847, Box 312, John Augustus Sutter Collection, California State Library, Sacramento, CA.

55. Sutter, *New Helvetia Diary*, 128; "T.M. Ames," *Daily Placer Times and Transcript* (Sacramento, CA), May 5, 1849.

56. "Prospects of the Gold Finders," *Ainsworth's Magazine* 15 (1849): 446.

57. Theodore T. Johnson, *Sights in the Gold Region, and Scenes by the Way* (New York: Baker and Scribner, 1849), 221.

58. *The Army Surveys of Gold Rush California: Reports of the Topographical Engineers, 1849–1851*, eds. Gary Clayton Anderson and Laura Lee Anderson (Norman: University of Oklahoma Press, 2015), 56–57.

59. Johann Sutter to Pearson Reading, January 29, 1846, Box 285, John Augustus Sutter Collection, California State Library, Sacramento, CA.

60. George McKinstry to John Bidwell, March 20, 1849, Sutter Fort Collection.

61. John Frederick Morse, *The First History of Sacramento City, 1853* (Sacramento, CA: Sacramento Books Collectors Club, 1945), 24.

62. *Army Surveys of Gold Rush California*, 56–57.

63. Eifler, *Gold Rush Capitalists*, 39.

64. "Sacramento City," *Placer Times* (Sacramento, CA), May 5, 1849.

65. Johann Sutter to Victor Prudon, January 1, 1846, Box 312, John Augustus Sutter Collection, California State Library, Sacramento, CA.

66. John Plumbe to James Gordon Bennet of the *New York Herald*, April 1851, in *The Settlers and Land Speculators of Sacramento* (New York, 1851), 29.

67. Morse, *First History of Sacramento City*, 26.

68. Edward Lehr, *Sutterville: The Unsuccessful Attempt to Establish a Town Safe from Floods* (Sacramento, CA: Sacramento State College, 1958), 50.

69. Lehr, *Sutterville*, 60.

70. Edmund Lorenzo Barber and George Holbrook Baker, *Sacramento Illustrated*, ed. Grant Dahlstrom, Caroline Wenzel and Jack Barrett (Sacramento, CA: Sacramento Book Collectors Club, 1950), 69–71.

71. "China Doctor," *Sacramento (CA) Bee*, February 25, 1857.

72. "Sacramento vs. Sutterville," *Nevada Democrat* (Nevada City, CA), January 21, 1862.

73. William T. Sherman, *Memoirs of General William T. Sherman* (New York: D. Appleton and Company, 1904), 105.

74. "Folsom or Sutterville," *Sacramento (CA) Age*, February 20, 1858.

75. "Historic Landsite," *Sacramento (CA) Bee*, February 20, 1947; "New Land Park Subdivision," *Sacramento (CA) Bee*, March 1, 1947.

Chapter 3

76. "New Town," *Sacramento Transcript*, May 9, 1850.

77. "For Sale, Town Lots in Brighton," *Sacramento Daily Union*, June 21, 1850.

78. "The Funeral of Mr. Woodland," *Sacramento Daily Union*, August 16, 1850.

79. Thomas J. Savage, "Emeline and Jeremiah," *California History* 93, no. 2, 41.

80. Thompson and West, *History of Sacramento County*, 211.

81. "The Celebration at Brighton," *Sacramento Transcript*, July 6, 1850.

82. Savage, "Emeline and Jeremiah," 41.

83. Statutes of 1851, Statutes of California, 2nd Session of the Legislature, Chapter 106, sec 1, 423.

84. "The Courts," *Sacramento Daily Union*, June 9, 1854.

85. Sacramento County Assessor, *Sacramento County Assessor Map Book, 1854*, 437, online at https://archive.org/details/SacCountyMapBook1870/page/n59/mode/2up.

86. The full collection is findable by searching for "Subdivision Map Book" at www.archive.org.

87. Sacramento County Assessor, *City of Sacramento Assessor Map Book, 1854*, 432–34, online at https://archive.org/details/sacramentocityma1854sacr/page/432/mode/2up.

88. Sacramento County Assessor, *City of Sacramento Assessor Map Book, 1854*, 437, online at https://archive.org/details/Co-SacCityMapBook1855/page/n437/mode/2up.

89. "Monte Vista!" *Sacramento Union*, May 3, 1888.

90. "In the Spring of '50," *Union*, August 8, 1892.

91. "The Fourth of July—The Pavilion," *Transcript*, July 2, 1850.

92. "Great Fire at Brighton," *Union*, October 13, 1852.

93. "Notice," *Union*, July 23, 1850.

94. "The Great Races," *Transcript*, May 20, 1851.

95. "Brighton Race Course," *Union*, February 7, 1852.

96. "Match Race at Brighton," *Union*, March 18, 1852.

97. "Proceedings of Last Night," *Transcript*, August 16, 1850.

98. "Sacramento's Early Days," *Union*, March 24, 1893.

99. "Brighton Eating House," *Daily Placer Times and Tribune*, October 13, 1849.

100. Savage, "Emeline and Jeremiah," 41.

101. Paula Peper, *Sacramento's Brighton Township: Stories of the Land* (Sacramento, CA: Stonebridge Properties LLC, 2009), 23.

102. Peper, *Sacramento's Brighton Township*, 33.

103. "Meeting of the Settlers of Brighton Township," *Union*, September 28, 1853.

104. "Contest Among Settlers," *Union*, December 14, 1854.

105. "Hanging in Effigy," *Union*, May 26, 1855.

106. "A Card," *Union*, February 7, 1857.

107. "A Serious Difficulty Brewing," *Bee*, July 18 1857.

108. William H. Gwinn, "The History of the Freeport Railroad, 1863–1865," History 101 paper, Sacramento State College, 1964, 3.

109. Gwinn, "History of the Freeport Railroad," 9.

110. Gwinn, "History of the Freeport Railroad," 21.

Chapter 4

111. Academic database searches using "Norristown" generally lead to the city in Pennsylvania. Combining that keyword with "Sacramento" returns mainly results in which the two place names are very loosely connected—often address lists.

112. Allen L. Chickering, "Samuel Norris: Litigious Pioneer," *California Historical Society Quarterly* 25, no. 3 (September 1946): 223.

113. William Dillinger, ed., *A History of the Lower American River* (Sacramento, CA: American River Natural History Association, 1991), 85.

114. USGS, *Brighton Quad* (1911), online at https://ngmdb.usgs.gov/topoview/viewer.

115. Kelley, *Battling the Inland Sea*, 157–74.

116. City of Sacramento, *Historical Growth by Annexation*, 2013.

117. Phinney, Cate & Marshall, *Map of Sacramento City* (1913), online at https://archive.org/details/mapofsacramentocity.

118. Search results in the *California Digital Newspaper Collection* drop precipitously after mid-1850, with most references being real estate notices using Norristown as a point of reference.

119. "Norristown," *Placer Times*, March 2, 1850.

120. "First Steamer on the American River, *Placer Times*, April 22, 1850.

121. "County Election," *Placer Times*, March 16, 1850.

122. "Election Notice," *Placer Times*, May 9, 1850.

123. "Orders No 2," *Transcript*, July 4, 1850.

124. California Historical Landmarks, "CHL No. 697 Pony Express Five Mile House—Sacramento," *California Historical Landmarks*.

125. "Sheriff's Sale," *Sacramento Daily Union*, October 29, 1855.

126. Lewis Sanders Jr. and William Muldrow, *Map of the Partition Between Sanders & Muldrow, in October 1858 and May 1860* (1860), California State Library, Sacramento, CA.

127. The Center for Sacramento History's collection of digitized volumes is available at https://archive.org.

128. Sacramento County Assessor, *Deed Book 180*, 455–56.

129. Cheryl Anne Stapp, *Before the Gold Rush* (Sacramento, CA: CreateSpace Independent Publishing Platform, 2017), 23.

130. Stapp, *Before the Gold Rush*, 77.

131. Stapp, *Before the Gold Rush*, 28.

132. USGS, *Brighton Quad* (1911), online at https://ngmdb.usgs.gov/topoview/viewer.

133. *Plat of Survey Showing Location of North-West Corner of "Norristown,"* online at http://assessorparcelviewer.saccounty.net.

134. This right-of-way's former intersection with the riverside levee is marked by a concrete wing wall, suggesting a road designed for heavy vehicles. The rail levee intersection is marked by a pair of trapezoidal soil features protruding from the gravel-clad levee; this would be consistent with a crossing being built but later removed.

135. The Sacramento County Assessor's Parcel Viewer website shows two intact property lines approaching from the south and southeast over long distances. These follow Norristown's southern boundary and another approach that connects the spot to the section line road now known as 65th Street. Available online at http://assessorparcelviewer.saccounty.net.

136. Sacramento County Assessor, *Parcel Viewer*, APN 008-0020-017 and 008-0020-015. Available online at http://assessorparcelviewer.saccounty.net.

137. Aerial photos from as early as 1928 reveal a stable channel at a date closer to the gold rush than to the present. This suggests a relatively unchanged stretch of river with a ford at the location of Sinclair's crossing.

138. Walter C. Frame, "Fire, Floods & Hoboken," *Golden Notes* 13, no. 3 (April 1967): 3.

139. Frame, "Fire, Floods & Hoboken," 12.

140. Frame, "Fire, Floods & Hoboken," 10.

141. "Board of Supervisors," *Union*, January 8, 1853.

142. "Trustee James H. Devine a Hot-Air Virtuoso," *Bee*, January 8, 1901.

143. "If This City Does Not Object Railroad Company May Use the East Levee," *Bee*, March 10, 1902.

144. "Early Days," *Union*, January 2, 1882.

145. "The Seasons of High Water," *Union*, December 9, 1885.

Chapter 5

146. Plimpton Collection, vol. 2 (Mormon Island).

147. "Whig County Nominating Convention," *Sacramento Union*, July 14, 1856.

148. Judy D. Tordoff, *The Evolution of California's Placer Mining Landscape: A View from Prairie City* (Sacramento: California Department of Transportation, 2004), 8.

149. Antonio Castaneda et al., "Natomas Company, 1851–1984," unpublished, Sacramento, CA, 1984, 15.

150. John Plimpton, *Collection*, Box 3, vol. 2 (Mormon Island).

151. Tordoff, *Evolution of California's Placer Mining Landscape*, 8–9.

152. Tordoff, *Evolution of California's Placer Mining Landscape*, 8–9.

153. Tordoff, *Evolution of California's Placer Mining Landscape*, 8–9.

154. Tordoff, *Evolution of California's Placer Mining Landscape*, 51.

155. Plimpton, *Collection*, Box 3, vol. 2 (Mormon Island).

156. Plimpton, *Collection*, Box 3, vol. 2 (Mormon Island).

157. Plimpton, *Collection*, Box 3, vol. 2 (Mormon Island).

158. Clarence Caesar, "An Historical Overview of the Development of Sacramento's Black Community, 1850–1983," master's thesis, California State University, Sacramento, 1983, 21.

159. Kenneth G. Goode, *California's Black Pioneers: A Brief Historical Survey* (Santa Barbara, CA: McNally and Lofton, 1973), 59.

160. Plimpton, *Collection*, Box 3, vol. 2 (Mormon Island).

161. Rinaldo Taylor, *Seeing the Elephant: Letters of R.R. Taylor, Forty-Niner* (Los Angeles, CA: Ritchie Press, 1951), 70, October 22, 1849.

162. Tordoff, *Evolution of California's Placer Mining Landscape*, 41.

163. Stanley Buder, *Pullman: An Experiment in Industrial Order and Community Planning, 1880–1930* (Oxford: Oxford University Press, 1967), 1–5.

164. Plimpton, *Collection*, Box 3, vol. 2 (Mormon Island).

165. Plimpton, *Collection*, Box 3, vol. 2 (Mormon Island).

166. John N. Wilson, *These Lonely Hills* (Placerville, CA: El Dorado County Historical Museum, 2006), 42.

167. Plimpton, *Collection*, Box 3, vol. 2 (Mormon Island).

168. "Letter to the Editor," *Sacramento Union*, January 24, 1853.

169. Rudolph Lapp, *Blacks in Gold Rush California* (New Haven, CT: Yale University Press, 1977), 52.

170. Plimpton, *Collection*, Box 3, vol. 2 (Mormon Island).

171. Plimpton, *Collection*, Box 3, vol. 2 (Mormon Island).

172. Plimpton, *Collection*, Box 3, vol. 2 (Mormon Island).

173. Plimpton, *Collection*, Box 3, vol. 2 (Mormon Island).

174. Plimpton, *Collection*, Box 3, vol. 2 (Mormon Island).

175. Plimpton, *Collection*, Box 3, vol. 2 (Mormon Island).

176. Plimpton, *Collection*, Box 3 (South Fork of the American River), vol. 1 (Junction to American Island).

177. Lapp, *Blacks in Gold Rush California*, 93.

178. Plimpton, *Collection*, Box 3, vol. 2 (Mormon Island).

179. Plimpton, *Collection*, Box 3, vol. 2 (Mormon Island).

180. Plimpton, *Collection*, Box 2 (Middle Fork of the American River), vol. 2 (10 Mile Ford to Junction).
181. Plimpton, *Collection*, Box 3, vol. 2 (Mormon Island).
182. Ellen Marie Snyder, "Innocents in a Worldly World: Victorian Children's Gravemarkers," *Cemeteries and Gravemarkers: Voices of American Culture* (n.d.): 11.
183. Taylor, *Seeing the Elephant*, 70.
184. Plimpton, *Collection*, Box 3, vol. 2 (Mormon Island).
185. Plimpton, *Collection*, Box 3, vol. 2 (Mormon Island).
186. Tordoff, *Evolution of California's Placer Mining Landscape*, 53–54.
187. Tordoff, *Evolution of California's Placer Mining Landscape*, 53–54.
188. Tordoff, *Evolution of California's Placer Mining Landscape*, 53–54.
189. "Ghost Towns of Salmon Falls, Negro Hill and Mormon Island Are Seen on Nearby Auto Trip," *Sacramento Bee*, December 25, 1935.
190. Plimpton, *Collection*, Box 3 (South Fork of the American River) vol. 5 (New York Ravine).
191. Plimpton, *Collection*, Box 3 (South Fork of the American River) vol. 3 (McCall Correspondence).
192. Plimpton, *Collection*, Box 3 (South Fork of the American River) vol. 3 (McCall Correspondence).
193. Plimpton, *Collection*, Box 3 (South Fork of the American River) vol. 3 (McCall Correspondence).
194. Plimpton, *Collection*, Box 3 (South Fork of the American River) vol. 3 (McCall Correspondence).
195. Plimpton, *Collection*, Box 3 (South Fork of the American River) vol. 3 (McCall Correspondence).
196. Plimpton, *Collection*, Box 3 (South Fork of the American River) vol. 3 (McCall Correspondence).
197. "African American Veterans Buried Near El Dorado Hills Remain Unknown, Little Honored," *Sacramento Bee*, June 11, 2014.
198. Eric Costa, *Gold and Wine* (Placerville, CA: El Dorado Winery Association, 2010), 60.
199. Kevin Knauss, *Benjamin Norton Bugbey* (Granite Bay, CA: Kevin Knauss, 2019), 262–65.
200. Knauss, *Benjamin Norton Bugbey*, 56–57.
201. Knauss, *Benjamin Norton Bugbey*, 56–57.
202. Knauss, *Benjamin Norton Bugbey*, 134–35.
203. Knauss, *Benjamin Norton Bugbey*, 222.
204. Knauss, *Benjamin Norton Bugbey*, 223–24.
205. Knauss, *Benjamin Norton Bugbey*, 227.
206. Knauss, *Benjamin Norton Bugbey*, 227.

207. Knauss, *Benjamin Norton Bugbey*, 262.

208. Knauss, *Benjamin Norton Bugbey*, 264–65.

209. M.M. Cleveland, "The Economics of Henry George: A Review Essay," *American Journal of Economics and Sociology* 71, no. 2 (2012): 498–511.

210. Carol Witham, *A Field Guide to the Mather Vernal Pools* (Sacramento: California Native Plant Society, 2004), 7.

211. Witham, *Field Guide to the Mather Vernal Pools*.

212. Tim Horner, "Salmon and Steelhead in the American River," Bushy Lake Restoration Project, California State University Sacramento, May 6, 2024, www.bushylake.com.

213. Bureau of Land Management, Pine Hill Preserve, May 6, 2024, www.pinehillpreserve.org.

Chapter 6

214. Rodman W. Paul, ed., *The California Gold Discovery: Sources, Documents, Accounts, and Memoirs Relating to the Discovery of Gold at Sutter's Mill* (Georgetown, CA: Talisman Press, 1966), 37.

215. Paul, *California Gold Discovery*, 41.

216. Paul, *California Gold Discovery*, 62.

217. Erwin G. Gudde, *Bigler's Chronicle of the West: The Conquest of California, Discovery of Gold, and Mormon Settlement as Reflected in Henry William Bigler's Diaries* (Berkeley: University of California Press, 1962), 101.

218. Kenneth J. Davies, *Mormon Gold: Mormons in the California Gold Rush, Contributing to the Development of California and the Monetary Solvency of Early Utah* (Salt Lake City, UT: Granite Mountain Publishing, 2010), 20.

219. Paul, *California Gold Discovery*, 130.

220. Kenneth N. Owens, *Gold Rush Saints: California Mormons and the Great Rush for Riches* (Spokane, WA: Arthur H. Clark Company, 2004), 125.

221. Plimpton, *Collection*, Box 3, vol. 2 (Mormon Island).

222. Gudde, *Bigler's Chronicle of the West*, 105.

223. David L. Bigler, ed., *The Gold Discovery Journal of Azariah Smith* (Salt Lake City: University of Utah Press, 1990), 36.

224. Davies, *Mormon Gold*, 28.

225. James S. Brown, *Giant of the Lord-Life of a Pioneer* (Salt Lake City, Utah: Bookcraft, 1960), 114.

226. "Gold Mine Found," *The Californian*, March 15, 1848.

227. "Gold," *California Star*, March 18, 1848.

228. Hubert Howe Bancroft, *History of California*, 7 vols. (San Francisco, CA: History Company, 1886–90), 6:56.

229. Davies, *Mormon Gold*, 36.

230. *California Star*, April 1, 1848.

231. Davies, *Mormon Gold*, 36.

232. *The Californian*, April 19, 1848.

233. *California Star*, April 22, 1848.

234. Davies, *Mormon Gold*, 36.

235. Bigler, *Gold Discovery Journal of Azariah Smith*, 115.

236. Plimpton, *Collection*, Box 3, vol. 2 (Mormon Island).

237. Plimpton, *Collection*, Box 3, vol. 2 (Mormon Island).

238. Brown, *Giant of the Lord-Life of a Pioneer*, 115.

239. Brown, *Giant of the Lord-Life of a Pioneer*, 115.

240. Colonel R.B. Mason, "Mason Report, August 17, 1848," Exec. Doc. 17, H.R. 31st Congress, 1st session, 1850.

241. Plimpton, *Collection*, Box 3, vol. 2 (Mormon Island).

242. Davies, *Mormon Gold*, 47–48.

243. Plimpton, *Collection*, Box 3, vol. 2 (Mormon Island).

244. Plimpton, *Collection*, Box 3, vol. 2 (Mormon Island).

245. Plimpton, *Collection*, Box 3, vol. 2 (Mormon Island).

246. Paul, *California Gold Discovery*, 130.

247. Plimpton, *Collection*, Box 3, vol. 2 (Mormon Island).

248. Plimpton, *Collection*, Box 3, vol. 2 (Mormon Island).

249. Plimpton, *Collection*, Box 3, vol. 2 (Mormon Island).

250. Plimpton, *Collection*, Box 3, vol. 2 (Mormon Island).

251. Plimpton, *Collection*, Box 3, vol. 2 (Mormon Island).

252. Plimpton, *Collection*, Box 3, vol. 2 (Mormon Island).

253. Plimpton, *Collection*, Box 3, vol. 2 (Mormon Island).

254. Plimpton, *Collection*, Box 3, vol. 2 (Mormon Island).

255. Plimpton, *Collection*, Box 3, vol. 2 (Mormon Island).

256. Plimpton, *Collection*, Box 3, vol. 2 (Mormon Island).

257. Plimpton, *Collection*, Box 3, vol. 2 (Mormon Island).

258. Plimpton, *Collection*, Box 3, vol. 2 (Mormon Island).

259. Plimpton, *Collection*, Box 3, vol. 2 (Mormon Island).

260. Plimpton, *Collection*, Box 3, vol. 2 (Mormon Island).

261. Plimpton, *Collection*, Box 3, vol. 2 (Mormon Island).

262. "Exchange Hotel," *Orangevale News*, May 2, 1963.

263. Plimpton, *Collection*, Box 3, vol. 2 (Mormon Island).

264. Lapp, *Blacks in Gold Rush California*, 50–51.

265. Plimpton, *Collection*, Box 3, vol. 2 (Mormon Island).

266. Plimpton, *Collection*, Box 3, vol. 2 (Mormon Island).

267. Plimpton, *Collection*, Box 3, vol. 2 (Mormon Island).

268. Plimpton, *Collection*, Box 3, vol. 2 (Mormon Island).

269. Lapp, *Blacks in Gold Rush California*, 112, 259.

270. Davies, *Mormon Gold*, 37.

271. Davies, *Mormon Gold*, 37.

272. Davies, *Mormon Gold*, 37.

273. "Ella Mighels, Noted Author, Dies in Bay City," *Sacramento Bee*, December 11, 1934.

274. "My Gold Rocker Cradle," *Every Woman*, September 1914.

275. "Aurora Esmeralda, Noted Author, Once Wrote for the Sacramento Union," *Sacramento Union*, July 8, 1931.

276. Plimpton, *Collection*, Box 3, vol. 2 (Mormon Island).

277. Plimpton, *Collection*, Box 3, vol. 2 (Mormon Island).

278. Plimpton, *Collection*, Box 3, vol. 2 (Mormon Island).

279. Plimpton, *Collection*, Box 3, vol. 2 (Mormon Island).

280. "Locals in Brief," *Folsom Telegraph*, April 30, 1887.

281. Plimpton, *Collection*, Box 3, vol. 2 (Mormon Island).

282. Plimpton, *Collection*, Box 3, vol. 2 (Mormon Island).

283. Plimpton, *Collection*, Box 3, vol. 2 (Mormon Island).

284. Plimpton, *Collection*, Box 3, vol. 2 (Mormon Island).

285. Plimpton, *Collection*, Box 3, vol. 2 (Mormon Island).

286. Plimpton, *Collection*, Box 3, vol. 2 (Mormon Island).

287. *Sacramento County Court of Sessions*, May 2, 1854.

288. Plimpton, *Collection*, Box 3, vol. 2 (Mormon Island).

289. "Fire at Mormon Island," *Alta California*, June 25, 1856.

290. Plimpton, *Collection*, Box 3, vol. 2 (Mormon Island).

291. Plimpton, *Collection*, Box 3, vol. 2 (Mormon Island).

292. "Fire in Mormon Island," *Placer Herald*, June 28, 1856.

293. "Fire at Mormon Island," *Alta California*, June 25, 1856.

294. "Fire in Mormon Island," *Placer Herald*, June 28, 1856.

295. Plimpton, *Collection*, Box 3, vol. 2 (Mormon Island).

296. Plimpton, *Collection*, Box 3, vol. 2 (Mormon Island).

297. Plimpton, *Collection*, Box 3, vol. 2 (Mormon Island).

298. Plimpton, *Collection*, Box 3, vol. 2 (Mormon Island).

299. Plimpton, *Collection*, Box 3, vol. 2 (Mormon Island).

300. "The Grape Crop," *Folsom Telegraph*, October 20, 1866.

301. *Historical Souvenir of El Dorado County California with Illustrations and Biographical Sketches of Its Prominent Men and Pioneers* (Oakland, CA: Paolo Sioli, 1883), 111.

302. *Historical Souvenir of El Dorado County California*, 111.

303. Plimpton, *Collection*, Box 3, vol. 2 (Mormon Island).

304. Costa, *Gold and Wine*, 60–61.

305. Costa, *Gold and Wine*, 60–61.
306. Costa, *Gold and Wine*, 60–61.
307. Costa, *Gold and Wine*, 60–61.
308. "Vineyards and Sons of Temperance," *Sacramento Union*, March 1, 1869.
309. "Vineyards and Sons of Temperance."
310. Costa, *Gold and Wine*, 62.
311. Plimpton, *Collection*, Box 3, vol. 2 (Mormon Island).
312. Plimpton, *Collection*, Box 3, vol. 2 (Mormon Island).

Chapter 7

313. Erwin Gudde, *California Place Names: The Origin and Etymology of Current Geographical Names*, 4th ed. (Berkeley: University of California Press, 1998), 258.
314. "CSM Professor, Activist Rudy Lapp Dies," *Daily Observer* (San Mateo, CA), May 30, 2007.
315. "Meetings," *California Historical Society Quarterly* 27, no. 1 (March 1948): 85, accessed October 11, 2020, https://www.jstor.org/stable/25156086.
316. *Historical Souvenir of El Dorado County California*, 201.
317. Lapp, *Blacks in Gold Rush California*, 51.
318. *Historical Souvenir of El Dorado County California*, 201.
319. James Williams, *Fugitive Slave in the Gold Rush: Life and Adventures of James Williams* (Lincoln: University of Nebraska Press, 2002), 22.
320. "Negro Hill," *Sacramento Daily Union*, January 14, 1852.
321. "Negro Hill," *Daily Alta California*, February 1, 1852.
322. *Historical Souvenir of El Dorado County California*, 201.
323. "Negro Hill," *Empire County Argus*, January 7, 1854.
324. *Historical Souvenir of El Dorado County California*, 201.
325. "December 26, 1854," Newton C. Miller Letters, BANC MSS C-B 807, Berkeley, Bancroft Library, University of California.
326. *Historical Souvenir of El Dorado County California*, 201.
327. Plimpton, *Collection*, Box 3 (South Fork of the American River) vol. 1 (Junction to American Island).
328. "Fare Reduced!" *Sacramento Daily Union*, November 22, 1854.
329. "A Stage Depot," *Sacramento Daily Union*, March 14, 1856.
330. "New Advertisements," *Chico Record*, December 14, 1857.
331. Plimpton, *Collection*, Box 3, vol. 1 (Junction to American Island).
332. Lapp, *Blacks in the California Gold Rush*, 51.
333. *Historical Souvenir of El Dorado County California*, 201.
334. Jack Wolf, introduction, in *Newton C. Miller Letters*, October 10, 1960.
335. "Convention of Water Companies," *Sacramento Daily Union*, October 4, 1853.

336. "December 12, 1853," in *Newton C. Miller Letters.*
337. "January 8th 1854," in *Newton C. Miller Letters.*
338. Wolf, introduction, in *Newton C. Miller Letters.*
339. "For the Nevada Journal," *Nevada Journal*, March 7, 1856.
340. Wolf, introduction, in *Newton C. Miller Letters.*
341. Wolf, introduction, in *Newton C. Miller Letters.*
342. "March 13, 1854," in *Newton C. Miller Letters.*
343. "March 13, 1854," in *Newton C. Miller Letters.*
344. "March 13, 1854," in *Newton C. Miller Letters.*
345. "December 26, 1854," in *Newton C. Miller Letters.*
346. "December 26, 1854," in *Newton C. Miller Letters.*
347. "December 26, 1854," in *Newton C. Miller Letters.*
348. "December 26, 1854," in *Newton C. Miller Letters.*
349. "December 26, 1854," in *Newton C. Miller Letters.*
350. Plimpton, *Collection*, Box 3, vol. 1 (Junction to American Island).
351. Plimpton, *Collection*, Box 3, vol. 1 (Junction to American Island).
352. *Historical Souvenir of El Dorado County California*, 202.
353. *Historical Souvenir of El Dorado County California*, 202.
354. "Great Excitement at Mormon Island," *Sacramento Union*, January 29, 1853.
355. "Great Excitement at Mormon Island," *Sacramento Union*, January 29, 1853.
356. "Fatal Stabbing Affray," *Sacramento Daily Union*, March 7, 1855.
357. "The Negro Hill Affray," *Sacramento Daily Union*, March 13, 1855.
358. "Mariposa Correspondence," *San Joaquin Republican*, April 1, 1855.
359. "Law Courts," *Daily Alta California*, February 14, 1852.
360. Shirley Moore, *Sweet Freedom's Plains: African Americans on the Overland Trails, 1841–1869* (Norman: University of Oklahoma Press, 2016), 160–62.
361. "Negro Hill Affray."
362. Plimpton, *Collection*, Box 3, vol. 1 (Junction to American Island).
363. "Important Arrest," *Trinity Journal*, April 28, 1855.
364. *Historical Souvenir of El Dorado County California*, 202.
365. Plimpton, *Collection*, Box 3, vol. 1 (Junction to American Island).
366. "District Court," *Empire County Argus*, January 28, 1854.
367. "District Court," *Empire County Argus*, February 4, 1854.
368. "Court of Sessions," *Sacramento Union*, November 16, 1857.
369. "Calendar Court of Sessions—January Term," *Sacramento Union*, January 14, 1859.
370. Knauss, *Benjamin Norton Bugbey*, 219.
371. Knauss, *Benjamin Norton Bugbey*, 219.
372. Plimpton, *Collection*, Box 3, vol. 1 (Junction to American Island).
373. Knauss, *Benjamin Norton Bugbey*, 219.

374. Lapp, *Blacks in the California Gold Rush*, 51–52.
375. Lapp, *Blacks in the California Gold Rush*, 51–52.
376. Plimpton, *Collection*, Box 3, vol. 1 (Junction to American Island).
377. "Negro Hill," *Folsom Telegraph*, November 16, 1860.
378. Plimpton, *Collection*, Box 3, vol. 1 (Junction to American Island).
379. "Removal of County Seat," *Georgetown News*, February 21, 1856.
380. "Location of the County Seat," *Georgetown News*, April 17, 1856.
381. Plimpton, *Collection*, Box 3, vol. 1 (Junction to American Island).
382. Plimpton, *Collection*, Box 3, vol. 1 (Junction to American Island).
383. Plimpton, *Collection*, Box 3, vol. 1 (Junction to American Island).
384. Plimpton, *Collection*, Box 3, vol. 1 (Junction to American Island).
385. Plimpton, *Collection*, Box 3, vol. 1 (Junction to American Island).
386. Plimpton, *Collection*, Box 3, vol. 1 (Junction to American Island).
387. "Ditch and Mining Enterprise," *Placer Herald*, August 26, 1876.
388. Plimpton, *Collection*, Box 3, vol. 1 (Junction to American Island).
389. Plimpton, *Collection*, Box 3, vol. 1 (Junction to American Island).
390. Plimpton, *Collection*, Box 3, vol. 1 (Junction to American Island).
391. Plimpton, *Collection*, Box 3, vol. 1 (Junction to American Island).
392. "Ghost Towns of Salmon Falls, Negro Hill and Mormon Island Are Seen on Nearby Auto Trip," *Sacramento Bee*, December 25, 1935.
393. "Teachers Picnic," *Folsom Telegraph*, May 28, 1953.

Chapter 8

394. "Prairie City Thrives Again at Dedication," *Folsom Telegraph*, November 10, 1950.
395. "Prairie City Thrives Again at Dedication."
396. "Prairie City Thrives Again at Dedication."
397. Plimpton, *Collection*, Box 2 (Middle Fork of the American River), vol. 2 (10 Mile Ford to Junction).
398. Tordoff, *Evolution of California's Placer Mining Landscape*, 41.
399. Plimpton, *Collection*, Box 2, vol. 2 (10 Mile Ford to Junction).
400. Plimpton, *Collection*, Box 2, vol. 2 (10 Mile Ford to Junction).
401. Tordoff, *Evolution of California's Placer Mining Landscape*, 9.
402. Thompson and West, *History of Sacramento County*, 225.
403. Sacramento County, *Sacramento County Assessor Rolls*, 1857.
404. "Prairie City" *Sacramento (Pictorial) Union*, April 1854.
405. Thompson and West, *History of Sacramento County*, 225.
406. Sacramento County, *Sacramento County Assessor Rolls*, 1857.
407. Tordoff, *Evolution of California's Placer Mining Landscape*, 11.
408. "Prairie City," *Sacramento Union*, June 22, 1853.

409. "Prairie City," *Sacramento Union*, July 4, 1853.

410. Thompson and West, *History of Sacramento County*, 225.

411. Wilson, *These Lonely Hills*, 54.

412. Plimpton, *Collection*, Box 2, vol. 2 (10 Mile Ford to Junction).

413. "Correspondence of the Union," *Sacramento Union*, November 23, 1853.

414. "Prairie City," *Sacramento (Pictorial) Union*, April 1, 1854.

415. Tordoff, *Evolution of California's Placer Mining Landscape*, 11.

416. Tordoff, *Evolution of California's Placer Mining Landscape*, 11.

417. Plimpton, *Collection*, Box 2, vol. 2 (10 Mile Ford to Junction).

418. Plimpton, *Collection*, Box 2, vol. 2 (10 Mile Ford to Junction).

419. Tordoff, *Evolution of California's Placer Mining Landscape*, 11.

420. Plimpton, *Collection*, Box 2, vol. 2 (10 Mile Ford to Junction).

421. Tordoff, *Evolution of California's Placer Mining Landscape*, 42.

422. Plimpton, *Collection*, Box 2, vol. 2 (10 Mile Ford to Junction).

423. Plimpton, *Collection*, Box 2, vol. 2 (10 Mile Ford to Junction).

424. Tordoff, *Evolution of California's Placer Mining Landscape*, 52.

425. Tordoff, *Evolution of California's Placer Mining Landscape*, 53.

426. Tordoff, *Evolution of California's Placer Mining Landscape*, 54.

427. Tordoff, *Evolution of California's Placer Mining Landscape*, 54.

428. Tordoff, *Evolution of California's Placer Mining Landscape*, 56–57.

429. Plimpton, *Collection*, Box 2, vol. 2 (10 Mile Ford to Junction).

430. "Vanished Prairie City," *Sacramento Union*, January 7, 1906.

431. Plimpton, *Collection*, Box 2, vol. 2 (10 Mile Ford to Junction).

Aftermath

432. "Trustee Sale of Sutter Title," *Union*, January 21, 1857.

433. "The Sutter Sale," *Union*, February 7, 1857.

434. "That Sale," *Union*, February 17, 1857.

435. "City Intelligence," *Union*, April 17, 1868.

436. "Ejectment Suits," *Union*, May 2, 1868.

437. Sacramento City Extension Homestead Association, *Articles of Association, Act of Incorporation, By-laws Etc.* (Sacramento, CA: H.S. Crocker & Company, 1869), 26.

438. Sacramento City Extension Homestead Association, *Articles of Association*, 5.

439. U.S. Geological Survey, *Sacramento Sheet*, 1893 ed., 30-Minute Series (Topographic) (Reston, VA: USGS, 1900), online at http://historicalmaps.arcgis.com/usgs.

440. City of Sacramento, *Historical Growth by Annexation*, 2013.

441. Eifler, *Gold Rush Capitalists*, 128–29.

INDEX

ABOUT THE AUTHORS

Andrew McLeod is a historian of Sacramento's early land struggles. His research explores the widespread and organized resistance to land claims rooted in Johann Sutter's fabricated Mexican grant, as well as that struggle's erasure from history. McLeod was born in Sacramento and now lives at what was once a watering hole along the Sutterville-Brighton Road and, more recently, Monte Vista—an 1880s commuter suburb with its own depot on California's original railroad line. He is on the cusp of graduation from the public history graduate program at Sacramento State University.

Eric Webb is a retired circulation supervisor for the Sacramento Public Library. He completed his undergraduate and graduate studies in history and humanities from Sacramento State University. He is coauthor of *World War II Sacramento* (The History Press, 2018) and resides in Sacramento with his wife and beloved native plant garden.

A native of Portland, Oregon, JAMES SCOTT is the archivist for the Sacramento Public Library, where he's worked since 2000, when he started as a librarian. Scott is a graduate of Marquette University and has master's degrees in German history from Portland State University and information science from San Jose State University. He has written books and articles on both saloon culture in gold rush–era Sacramento and total war and aviation/aerospace defense in the capital region. Scott lives in East Sacramento and North Portland with his wife, son and a black and tan Dachshund named Schweinsteiger.

Set in the original 1918 Carnegie Foundation–funded section of the Sacramento Public Library, the SACRAMENTO ROOM was founded in 1995 as an archives and special collections for primary and secondary research materials relative to the history of the Sacramento region. Its rare book, book art, map, city directory, photograph, digital and manuscript collections make it one of the premier spots for historical research in Northern California. The Sacramento Room can be visited online at https://www.saclibrary.org.

Visit us at
www.historypress.com